Madame Butterfly

AND

A Japanese Nightingale

Madame Butterfly

JOHN LUTHER LONG

AND

A Japanese Nightingale

ONOTO WATANNA
(WINNIFRED EATON)

•

Two Orientalist Texts

EDITED BY
MAUREEN HONEY
AND JEAN LEE COLE

Rutgers University Press
New Brunswick, New Jersey, and London

Library of Congress Cataloging-in-Publication Data

Long, John Luther, 1861–1927.

Madame Butterfly / John Luther Long and A Japanese nightingale / Onoto Watanna (Winnifred Eaton) : two Orientalist texts / edited and with an introduction by Maureen Honey and Jean Lee Cole.

p. cm.

Includes bibliographical references (p.).

ISBN 0-8135-3062-8 (cloth: alk. paper) — ISBN 0-8135-3063-6 (pbk. : alk. paper)

1. Japan—Fiction. I. Honey, Maureeen, 1945– II. Cole, Jean Lee. III. Watanna, Onoto, 1879–1954. Japanese nightingale. IV. Title.

PS3523.O4685 M33 2002

813'.4—dc21   *2001048400*

British Cataloging-in-Publication information is available from the British Library.

Manufactured in the United States of America

Frontispiece. From Madame Butterfly *by John Luther Long (New York: Century, 1898). Illustrated by C. D. Weldon.*

For Diana Birchall

Contents

Illustrations

Acknowledgments

WE wish to thank the many people who helped make this publication possible. First of all, we thank Diana Birchall, Winnifred Eaton's granddaughter and biographer, for her belief that *A Japanese Nightingale* should be reprinted and that we were appropriate editors of such a project. Without her encouragement, we may not have pursued this work with such vigor and confidence. Other descendents of Winnifred Eaton have been equally generous with their information and encouragement, especially Elizabeth and Tim Rooney, who shared family stories with us in Montreal and took us, along with Diana, to the Eaton gravesite. For his astute reading of the proposal for this book, we thank as well Min Song. His comments immeasurably improved the introduction and pointed us in directions that were fruitful to follow. Mari Yoshihara and Michael Winship provided invaluable feedback in the early stages of our introduction. Enthusiastic interest in this project from Dominika Ferens and Allison Faust is also deeply appreciated. Our editor at Rutgers, Leslie Mitchner, demonstrated bracing confidence in this project and shepherded our proposal and manuscript through the editorial process with great efficiency and foresight. Other editors at Rutgers also deserve credit for the professional quality of this book, most especially Marilyn Campbell and Theresa Liu. Our thanks go as well to the Research Council at the University of Nebraska for funding this project.

Many scholars of Asian American literature and history have paved the way for our contextualization of Winnifred Eaton's novel. Most notable have been Lisa Botshon, Roger Daniels, Dominika Ferens, Elaine Kim, Robert G. Lee, Shirley Geok-Lin Lim, Lisa Lowe, Gina Marchetti, Yuko Matsukawa, Linda Trinh Moser, Samina Najmi, Eve Oishi, Gary Okihiro, Pat Shea, Ronald Takaki, Annette White-Parks, William F. Wu. Above all, we owe a debt of gratitude to the late Amy Ling, whose pioneering research on the Eaton sisters began a late twentieth-century revival of interest in their contributions to the Asian American literary tradition. Hiroko Sato is another pioneering scholar who helped pave the way for this volume and whose comments at our panel for the Montreal American Studies Association pointed us toward important points in our discussion of Eaton.

Our gratitude also goes to Sheri Tornatore for her artistic vision in designing the cover of this book, University of Nebraska graduate assistants

Jeannine Nyangira and Michael Medwick for scanning and editing Long's and Eaton's texts, and Apollonia Steele, archivist of Winnifred Eaton's papers at the University of Calgary, for helping us locate documents regarding the staging of *A Japanese Nightingale* and other papers relevant to the novel. As well we wish to thank people at the Harry Ransom Humanities Research Center at the University of Texas-Austin who helped us locate material in the John Luther Long Collection and to Dr. Kevin Lavender for his help in locating some of the images for this edition at the University of North Texas. All of their assistance was instrumental in making this a better book.

Finally, we wish to extend our deep appreciation to Matt Cole and Tom Kiefer for their indispensable support through various stages of this project. Their daily understanding and generosity helped us keep our balance and maintain rather daunting work schedules until we arrived at the finish line.

Madame Butterfly

AND

A Japanese Nightingale

Introduction

THE two short novels included in this volume, John Luther Long's *Madame Butterfly* (1898) and Winnifred Eaton's *A Japanese Nightingale* (1901), written under the pseudonym Onoto Watanna, appeared at the height of the American fascination with Japanese culture. Although "things Japanese" had been fashionable in Europe, and especially France, since Commodore Matthew Perry established diplomatic relations there in 1854, American interest was only sparked in 1876, with the publicity surrounding the Japanese Pavilion featured at the Philadelphia Centennial Exhibition. The American admiration for Japanese handicrafts reached its height with the widespread media coverage of the Japanese exhibits at the 1893 World's Fair in Chicago; at almost the same time, the United States witnessed Japan's impressive defeat of the Chinese in the 1894–1895 Sino-Japanese War. In the popular press, Americans referred to the Japanese as "the Yankees of the East"; one writer declared that "everybody wanted to know, and knowing, liked the Japs."[1]

By the late 1890s, Americans of all income levels furnished their homes with Japanese-style furniture, bought decorative lacquerware and painted screens, and devoured both fiction and nonfiction treating Japan and the supposedly quaint, exotic people who lived there. Most popular of these texts were William Elliott Griffis's *The Mikado's Empire* (1880), Basil Hall Chamberlain's *Things Japanese* (1905), and the numerous works of Lafcadio Hearn. Other books described *Japanese Girls and Women* (1891) and *Japanese Homes and Their Surroundings* (1885). The proliferation of writing about Japan was such that Chamberlain quipped in 1905, "it may be inferred that *not* to have written a book about Japan is fast becoming a title to distinction" (64).

---

[1] Qtd. in LaFeber, 50. Of course, not all Americans were equally enamored of the refinements of Japanese culture, and many found Japanese imperialistic exploits threatening to American interests—for them, Japan replaced China as the "Yellow Peril." LaFeber argues that blatantly negative attitudes toward the Japanese did not become the dominant view until the first decade of the twentieth century, whereas fellow historian Joseph M. Henning argues that pro- and anti-Japanese views coexisted throughout the period (LaFeber, 55–64, and Henning, chap. 6).

Long and Eaton exploited this fad for "Japonica." Although neither writer had ever been to Japan, they were both acquainted with the country's culture and customs by association: Long's sister had spent twenty years there as the wife of a missionary, whereas Eaton's English father had traveled to Japan and China as a representative of his family's textile business during the 1860s (he met his Chinese wife, Grace Trefusis, during his travels and married her in Shanghai).

For half-Chinese Eaton, the surprising and anomalous popularity of the Japanese in America—in contrast to the view that Chinese civilization was barbaric, unevolved, and destined for extinction—eased her access into a literary career during a time of often virulent racism. She used her slightly Asian appearance to validate her authorial identity as Onoto Watanna, who, according to a widely published biographical account, was raised in Japan and descended from both Japanese and English nobility. Eaton's older sister, Edith, was also a writer, but chose to embrace her maternal Chinese heritage rather than "pass" for Japanese, as Winnifred did; writing under the pseudonym Sui Sin Far, Edith was recognized for her advocacy of Chinese immigrants, but remained virtually unknown to the broader American public.[2] Thus, although Long and Eaton chose to write about Japan because of its marketability, Eaton had the added motivation of using Japan as a screen for her own problematic identity.

Indeed, although their writings were similar in many ways—the two even accused each other of plagiarism at various points in their careers—Long and Eaton could not have been more different. Born in Montreal, the Eurasian Eaton was the eighth of fourteen children, and struggled throughout her life to support both herself and her family. She received little formal education due to financial circumstances; she left her family at the age of eighteen, and within a period of less than a year, took a position as a journalist in faraway Jamaica, then moved to Chicago, where she shared a room at the YWCA and worked in the stockyards as a stenographer while writing the manuscript for what would become her first novel, the first written in English by a person of Asian descent, *Miss Numè of Japan* (1899). Throughout her career, which extended through the 1920s, Eaton worked incessantly, struggling not just to achieve fame but

---

[2] For more about Edith, see Annette White-Parks's informative *Sui Sin Far/Edith Maude Eaton: A Literary Biography* (1995). Dominika Ferens provides a more balanced, if less comprehensive, account in *Edith and Winnifred Eaton: The Uses of Ethnography in Turn-of-the-Century Asian American Literature* (2002). Edith's works are published in *Mrs. Spring Fragrance and Other Writings (1912),* ed. Amy Ling and Annette White-Parks (1995).

to make enough money to keep herself—and later, her husband and four children—fed, clothed, and housed.[3]

Long, in contrast, came from a respected and established family in Ashbourne, Pennsylvania, just outside of Philadelphia. Well educated, he led a comfortable existence as a lawyer, devoted husband, and father. He spent the summers with his wife and son at their resort house in Spray Beach, New Jersey, where he ostensibly devoted himself to his writing, but had a reputation as "the laziest man in town," and was "ever ready to contribute his share to the social enjoyment of the little summer colony of cottagers."[4] If Eaton exemplified the upwardly-striving, hardworking immigrant daughter, Long embodied the late nineteenth-century values of what T. J. Jackson Lears describes as "the moral and intellectual leaders of the American WASP bourgeoisie" (xiv). Troubled by the seeming "non-morality" of burgeoning consumer culture, upper-class Americans like Long appealed to premodern cultures—in particular, the chivalric code of medieval Europe and the orderly militarism of shogunate Japan—to relocate a moral center. The appeal of Japan, according to Lears, ranged from the utter calm and selfless spirituality offered by Buddhist notions of nirvana, to the dainty yet sexualized femininity that provided a "negative identity" against which the American male could demonstrate his vitality and virility (225–241).[5] Long expressed both of these attitudes in his writing: although *Madame Butterfly* exposed "the cruelty of the Western point of view," as one reviewer maintained, the self-annihilation of the ever-faithful, ever-feminine Butterfly still emphasizes the manly dominance of the "disturbing foreigner" Pinkerton.[6]

Perhaps because it so effectively bridged the contradictory and competing views of the Japanese, Long's story, which was first published in the highly respected *Century Illustrated Magazine* in January 1898, took hold of the American imagination. Long's first novel, *Miss Cherry-*

---

[3] Eaton recounted, in sensational style, her experiences as a young aspiring writer in her semi-autobiographical novel, *Me* (1915), which has been edited by Linda Trinh Moser and reprinted by the University of Mississippi Press (1998). For a more grounded factual account of Eaton's early life, one written by her granddaughter, see Diana Birchall's biography *Onoto Watanna: The Story of Winnifred Eaton* (2001).

[4] *Ladies' Every Saturday*, October 5, 1895, 19. Clipping in the John Luther Long Papers, Harry Ransom Humanities Research Center, University of Texas-Austin, box 18, folder 4.

[5] In his study, Lears focuses on three figures: William Sturgis Bigelow, Percival Lowell, and George Cabot Lodge. His attempt to link these three men's interest in Japan to their personal attitudes toward patriarchal authority is less compelling than his analysis of their actual engagement with Japanese culture.

[6] Quotes taken from "This Week's Play Bills," *Washington Post*, November 16, 1906.

Blossom of Tokyo (1895), sold well and was positively reviewed, but it was *Madame Butterfly* that would be his claim to fame. Readers identified with the tragic figure of Cho-Cho-San, the girlish, sentimental geisha who falls in love with the "foreign devil," B. F. Pinkerton, not realizing that Pinkerton has married her purely on a whim. Like his real-life counterparts stationed in Japan, Pinkerton believes this is a "marriage for jus' liddle while," as it came to be known in the popular press—in effect, a temporary contract of concubinage between an American sojourner in Japan and a Japanese woman. Believing that Cho-Cho-San is "dainty, vivid, eager, formless material" expressly intended to conform to "his most wantonly whimsical wish" (75), he "marries," impregnates, and then abandons her, saying in "his own oblique way" that he will return "when the robins nested again" (43). For three years, Cho-Cho-San faithfully waits and raises their son, refusing even to consider the possibility that Pinkerton has simply discarded her. Every spring, she prepares the house for Pinkerton's expected return, waiting all night for him to appear. It is not until Pinkerton does return—with his new American wife—that she understands she has been betrayed, and attempts to kill herself. For she has been taught, in the samurai tradition, that one must "die with Honor / When one can no longer live with Honor" (92).

Long's story was brought to the attention of the theatrical impresario David Belasco, who adapted it for the stage in 1900. Although it was merely a "playlet," a short piece intended to follow the main program, *Madame Butterfly* became one of Belasco's greatest successes. Its primary innovation was its use of stagecraft—scenery and lighting—to depict the Japanese setting, and also Belasco's decision to indicate the length and anguish of Cho-Cho-San's vigil by directing his actress, Blanche Bates, to hold the attention of the audience for a full fourteen minutes in complete silence, with only changes in lighting to indicate the passage of time. He later remarked that "to keep an audience's imagination stirred—to persuade it that what it was witnessing was real—it was necessary to have a scene of changing beauty. There was not a dissenting voice in the criticism of that scene. My experiment was hazardous, but it succeeded" (7).

It certainly did. Giacomo Puccini, who attended the British premiere of the one-act play later that year, was so moved by this scene that he was inspired to compose what would become his most famous opera. The story that Puccini told in *Madama Butterfly*, which premiered at La Scala in 1904, is the version that people today are most familiar with—so familiar that David Henry Hwang felt it unnecessary to see the opera or read its libretto when writing his "deconstructivist" version of the opera, *M.*

Butterfly (1986). He wrote: "I didn't even know the plot of the opera!
... Yet, I felt convinced that the libretto would include yet another lotus
blossom pining away for a cruel Caucasian man, and dying for her love.
Such a story has become too much of a cliché not to be included in the ar-
chetypal East-West romance that started it all" (95).

In fact, however, it was Long's, not Puccini's version that narratively established the tragedy of Madame Butterfly, and Long himself was influenced by earlier nineteenth-century writers such as Pierre Loti and
Lafcadio Hearn, whose Japanese tales also depicted doll-like, tragic
geishas fatally enamored of Western men who abandon them for women
of their own race. As William Wu, Robert Lee, Gina Marchetti, and others have noted, Asian women in literature and film have most often been
stereotyped as "dragon ladies" or as "Butterflies"—they are either mysterious and malevolent seductresses or silent, passive victims of the patriarchal demimonde, succumbing to disease, suicide, or homicide. Whether
dragon lady or Butterfly, biracial love affairs between Western men and
Asian women in fiction almost always end unhappily, with violence, disease, and death befalling one or both main characters. The Butterfly narrative in particular marginalizes Asian women as prostitutes, concubines,
and tragic victims, while engendering notions of Western domination
and superiority.

A *Japanese Nightingale* contributed to the development of the Butterfly stereotype in some ways, but Eaton's novel provided an important
bridge between racialized cultural tropes at the turn of the century and
our present-day literature of ethnic solidarity and identity. For this reason
we have reprinted *Nightingale* for the first time since its original publication and paired it with Long's iconic text to illustrate Eaton's significant
revision of the tragic geisha figure, self-destructively enamored of her
American paramour. Popular enough in its own day to make Eaton a
celebrity, *Nightingale*, along with Eaton's nine other Japanese novels, has
languished in the dustbin of literature.[7] When her romances are reviewed

---

[7] A *Japanese Nightingale* was Eaton's second novel and published by Harper and Bros.;
it was translated into at least four languages, made into a Broadway play, and produced as
a silent film (in 1918). Eaton later claimed it sold over two hundred thousand copies, although no sales figures have survived to verify that number. Reviews of the novel were positive for the most part and appeared in *Harper's Weekly*, the *New York Times*, *Current
Literature*, the *New York Tribune*, *The Dial*, *The Athenaeum*, *Literary World*, and other
venues. No less a respected critic than William Dean Howells said of Eaton's story: "There
is a quite indescribable freshness in the art of this pretty novelette . . . which is like no other
art except in the simplicity which is native to the best art everywhere. . . . It has its little

by contemporary critics, they are often faulted for their infantilization of
Japanese heroines who fall in love with representatives of white male superiority and Western colonization: diplomats, businessmen, ministers,
and teachers.[8] Although praised for her marketing savvy and chameleon-
like authorial transformations, Eaton's fiction has not worn well, and it
seems to reinforce the nativist values of her day more than it challenges
them.[9]

Central to any interpretation of Eaton's work, however, is her position
as the first Asian American novelist, facing the demands of a racist, patriarchal publishing industry and pioneering a path from Orientalist caricature to humanized images of Asians. As Patricia Wald points out, the
contradictory nature of American citizenship and American authorship
forced writers in Eaton's time to "choose between conforming to cultural
prescriptions and refusing comprehensibility altogether" (2). As a mixed-
race woman, Eaton, like her heroine, Yuki, was considered by most
Americans to be a "mongrel," subhuman and incapable of reason, let alone
art. By adopting the guise of the geisha, the Butterfly, Eaton could at least
gain the ear, if not the full understanding, of her American audience. Her
decision to screen her identity and her writing behind conventions that
now strike present-day readers as offensive is ironic to say the least.

Looking deeper, we can also consider the ways in which Eaton used the
conventions of the Orientalist Japanese romance for her own ends. In
their studies of popular romantic fiction, Janice Radway, Hazel Carby,
and Jane Tompkins have shown how generic conventions both support
the male-dominated social order and provide a vehicle for change; romance writers and readers simultaneously uphold patriarchal narratives
and subvert them. Taking a different tack, Houston Baker has shown how
African American writers such as Charles Chesnutt and Booker T. Wash-

---

defects, but its directness, and sincerity, and its felicity through the sparing touch make me
unwilling to note them. In fact, I have forgotten them." "A Psychological Counter-Current
in Recent Fiction," *North American Review* 173 (1901): 880–881.

[8] Fairly typical of this criticism are Amy Ling's early comments about the Eaton sisters,
in which she contrasts Winnifred's Japanese novels unfavorably with Edith's Chinese stories:
"Without Edith's work for contrast, we would be less aware that Winnifred's novels, set in
Japan and relating stories of romance between charming Japanese or Japanese Eurasian girls
and Anglo men, reflected the taste of the day, exploiting stereotypes of the childlike female
and the fatherly, powerful male" (1987).

[9] Revisionist criticism of Winnifred Eaton's work is beginning to appear. In addition to
Linda Trinh Moser's afterword to the reprint of *Me* (1998), see Eve Oishi's introduction to
Miss Numè of Japan (1999) and Samina Najmi's introduction to *The Heart of Hyacinth*
(2000). Also see Cole, Ferens, and Hattori.

ington manipulated the conventions of racism so thoroughly that they could put their white readers "through changes" without their realization of it (46–47). Until recently, the cultural nationalism guiding much of Asian American literary scholarship has resulted in the wholesale rejection of texts like *A Japanese Nightingale,* which fail to depart radically from dominant (white) forms and ideologies. Yet we need to include them in this literary history if we are ever to gain a full understanding of the Asian American experience, particularly since many early stereotypes with which a writer like Eaton had to contend are still with us.

To take one of many examples of how Eaton subverts the archetypes she uses in her texts, the fact that we see Yuki from the vantage-point of others, primarily that of the American heir to a shipping fortune, Jack Bigelow, seems to minimize her agency and consciousness. She is seemingly objectified by Jack's Occidental male gaze, reduced to a childish plaything on the one hand or an adventuress out only for his money on the other. Her fractured English baby-talk, crouching postures, wheedling requests for cash, and sexual aggressiveness seem to cast Yuki as the classic dragon lady or Butterfly of Orientalist lore, especially in the narrative lacunae that erase her thoughts from the text. Throughout the novel, the narrator speaks through Jack, sees through Jack's eyes, and thinks Jack's thoughts.

It is possible, however, to read this narrative focus on Jack in a different way. Although we are now accustomed to ethnic writing that delves into the depths of a character like Yuki with observation of her inner states and motivations, such was not the case a hundred years ago. At that time, ethnic characters existed in literature largely as types: the black mammy, the Chinese laundryman or railyard cook, the Irish cop. And most (white) readers were perfectly content to leave them that way; they were not particularly interested in seeing the world from an Asian or African American viewpoint. In fact, they may have greatly resisted being asked to do so. Moreover, people of mixed race like Yuki at the turn of the century were considered aberrations, freaks of nature. Because of the mingling of racial genes in their blood, they were often assumed to be mentally or physically deformed.

By placing the narrative consciousness of *A Japanese Nightingale* in a sympathetic young man—a distinctly and admirably *American* young man—Eaton was able to expose her readers to a new perspective in a "safe" way and get around some of the problems she faced with Yuki's necessarily stereotyped presentation. Readers, like Jack, could be initially mystified, yet charmed by the geisha, grow to love her as Jack does, and celebrate Jack's final reunion with her. Although mixed-race marriages were regarded with horror in many quarters—and were even illegal in many states—the readers of Eaton's novel did not appear to react negatively toward the marriage between Yuki and Bigelow, in part because Eaton so successfully created an identification between them and her white male character. Through Jack, the reader can see what was so lovable about Yuki—or rather, could understand how it would feel to love someone like her.[10]

In contrast, Long quickly establishes Pinkerton's lack of sympathy with Cho-Cho-San and then removes him promptly from the scene. Pinkerton ridicules her religion, family, and culture while demanding that Cho-Cho-San cater to his every whim. He isolates her from any source of protection available to her in Japan, then abandons her forever after only three months. We see nothing more of Pinkerton, and the bulk of the story is told through a third-person narration of discussions between Cho-Cho-San and her maid, Suzuki, which are rendered in a tortured English dialect. Cho-Cho-San speaks English because Pinkerton has forbidden her to speak Japanese in his house and, even though he is no longer present, she insists to her maid that they obey his command so that the Eurasian child she has borne will speak the language of his father. The dialogues and soliloquies that make up the bulk of *Madame Butterfly* are painfully difficult to read one hundred years later, not only because the dialect is constructed through the artistic lens of an author who had never heard a Japanese speak English, but because it is infused by Cho-Cho-San's self-denigrating obsession with Pinkerton's love. Her life has no meaning outside of his gaze. Ironically, then, Eaton's substitution of Jack Bigelow's perspective for Cho-Cho-San's isolated torment empowers Yuki and renders her more human because her fractured English is kept to a minimum, while it is Jack's torment over her mysterious disappearances and prevarications that assumes center stage. He is at her mercy rather than the other way around.

It is important to recognize as well the significant rewriting Eaton accomplishes of the first text establishing the Butterfly myth, Pierre Loti's

---

[10] In his 1901 review, Howells succumbed completely to Yuki's attractions. He wrote that "the charm, the delight, the supreme interest [in the novel] is in the personality of Yuki"—a personality, he decides, that is of "surpassing lovableness." One of the most difficult things to understand about Howells's review is his apparent failure to recognize the stereotypical nature of Yuki's character. How could he *not* recognize it as such? The only way we can resolve this question is to locate Howells's reaction in Eaton's narrative strategy: he adopts Jack's sympathetic interest in Yuki as his own.

Madame Chrysanthème (1887), a widely read, fictionalized account of Loti's three-month marriage to a Japanese woman in Nagasaki while a lieutenant in the French navy.[11] Long and Eaton were undoubtedly familiar with this story as it enjoyed wide readership, went through twenty-five editions in only five years, and was translated into English as well as other languages. Virulently anti-Japanese and largely dismissive of his temporary wife's culture and humanity, Loti's story furnished the major characters, plot line, and setting for Long's and Eaton's relatively enlightened revisions a decade later.

The callous Pinkerton of Long's 1898 text is very much in keeping with the French lieutenant of *Madame Chrysanthème*, who habitually refers to Japanese as monkeys, rats, and immoral wretches who mimic civilization but who have little capacity for thought or feeling. His intention to marry a Japanese woman while he is in port at Nagasaki for three months is couched in classic exploitative terms: "I should take her for what she is: a fantastic and charming plaything. What an amusing little household I should set up! Really, short of marrying a china ornament, I should find it difficult to choose better" (46). When the lieutenant narrator of Loti's novel first sees a prospective Japanese bride only a few days after his arrival during the "look-at meeting" arranged by a go-between, he declares: "Long before setting foot in Japan, I had met with her, on every fan, on every tea-cup—with her silly air, her puffy little visage, her tiny eyes, mere gimlet-holes above those expanses of impossible pink and white which are her cheeks. She is young, that is all I can say in her favor" (56). Even when he agrees to marry the seventeen-year-old Chrysanthème instead, after rejecting this first selection with grotesque rudeness, he describes his new wife as having "*almost* an expression, *almost* a thought. . . . There is actually some expression in her glance, and I am *almost* persuaded that she—this one—thinks" (emphasis added; 59, 63). Far from regretting his racist contempt for the Japanese people with whom he lives during the summer before leaving for China on his ship, Loti's lieutenant is only too glad to be rid of them when he says goodbye: "At the moment of my departure, I can only find within myself a smile of careless mockery

---

[11] Jan van Rij indicates that the Butterfly myth was based in part on a historical reality in Japan after Matthew Perry's gunboat diplomacy forced economic contact between the Japanese and European powers in 1854. He describes as commonplace at the end of the nineteenth century the temporary marriages of Western sailors and Japanese young women, arrangements that were most often made with economically desperate women, whose reputations were permanently ruined by such liaisons (18–19).

for the swarming crowd of this Liliputian curtseying people,—laborious, industrious, greedy of gain, tainted with a constitutional affectation, hereditary insignificance, and incurable monkeyishness" (328).

Long wished to revise Loti's story in a way that created sympathy for the abandoned young woman, so he picked it up where the original ends—with the lieutenant's departure—in order to dramatize the tragic consequences of Western men using Japanese women as temporary playthings. His revisionist impulses went even further in a letter he wrote to the editor of *Century Magazine* two months after the sensational publication of *Madame Butterfly*. In it he proposed to write a story about an American man who "marries" a married Japanese woman as a way for her husband to repay a debt he owes the American and then truly falls in love with her; she, in turn, falls in love with him. However, through a variety of circumstances, the woman, like Butterfly, commits suicide at the end of the story.[12] In neither case, nor in any of his other Japanese stories, however, did Long go as far as Eaton did in her revision of Loti's racist text. Rather than replicate a doomed Asian woman who tragically pines away for her lost American love, she revises Long's story, as well as Loti's.

At first glance, *A Japanese Nightingale* appears to be yet another iteration of the Orientalist fantasy exoticized and eroticized by its predecessors. This impression is due to the many elements it shares with Long's text. A young geisha (Butterfly is seventeen; Yuki is sixteen) from an old samurai family is sold into marriage with an American to support a widowed mother; after living on a hill overlooking a major city and bay, the lovers separate after a few months and remain apart for two or three years; the marriage broker tries to sell the young woman again to another wealthy suitor; the geisha-heroine is an outcast in Japanese society and a sense of tragedy infuses both texts; other Americans bring the lovers back into contact with one another, with American women playing small but key roles in both stories; both texts employ the same pidgin dialect and infantilized speech patterns.

---

[12] This story, which Long tentatively titled "The Pink Geisha," is alluded to in the opening chapter of *Madame Butterfly*. Long anticipated the story's rejection, writing, "Now this seems daring, of course. But if the Eastern atmosphere is sufficiently retained, so that the reader will be in Japan, and not in America while he reads, and if the story is told with delicacy and refinement as it can be, it ought not to be offensive." The magazine's editor, R. W. Gilder, disagreed. In his response, he simply wrote, "I can see how the enclosed 'lay out' attracts you—But I am sorry—for it is questionable whether Jap [sic] ideas can be instilled into American minds." Letter in the John Luther Long Papers, box 8, folder 6.

Indeed, the narratives are so similar that Eaton and Long accused each other of plagiarism, charges that swirled around the opening of David Belasco's second Japanese play, *The Darling of the Gods*, in the fall of 1903, just before the stage version of *A Japanese Nightingale* opened in December of that year. Long had collaborated with Belasco on that production, as he had on *Madame Butterfly* in 1900, and Eaton was irked that the duo eclipsed her own Broadway debut with a script strikingly similar to *The Wooing of Wistaria* (1902), a novel she had sent to Belasco as possible play material, along with *A Japanese Nightingale*.

With the encouragement of the producers who staged *Nightingale*, she brought suit against Belasco. In an almost unbelievable turn of events that demonstrated Belasco's capacity for theatricality, he had her arrested on the opening night of *The Darling of the Gods*, and later sued her for libel.[13] When interviewed by the *New York Sunday Telegraph* about the controversy and Long's charges that she had lifted *Nightingale* from *Madame Butterfly*, Eaton frostily replied:

The Belasco affair is as absurd as the retaliation of Mr. Long, who claims that my work is copied from his. Naturally, when I decided to enter the literary world, I wanted to adopt a style of work that might be considered characteristic, and to labor in a field that was not overcrowded. Where could I turn for more interesting copy than my native country? To say that a Japanese woman copied the style of a man who probably did not see her country . . . is . . . absurd. . . . I am told Mr. Long is forty-five years old, and has written a volume of short stories. I am in the early twenties and have published six novels. At this rate, Mr. Long would not last me any length of time for inspirations.[14]

Eaton's vigorous denial of Long's plagiarism accusation grew out of a valid observation that both were working in the same cultural environment. At the same time, numerous aspects of plot, setting, and character that coincide with Long's text suggest she had more than a casual

---

[13] In the end, writes Birchall, the matter was settled with the order of arrest vacated in court. Birchall relates that Eaton's lawsuit against Belasco did not prevent *The Darling of the Gods* from overshadowing the dramatic version of *A Japanese Nightingale*, a dismal failure. The film version of *Nightingale* (1918) was similarly unsuccessful.

[14] "Jap Artist Sees 'A Japanese Nightingale,'" *New York Sunday Telegraph*, November 29, 1903. Birchall notes that Eaton misrepresented herself in several ways during this interview: she was not Japanese, nor had she ever seen Japan; she was twenty-eight when she made this statement, not in her early twenties; and she had published only four novels, not six.

acquaintance with the narrative, just as Long echoed Loti's plot elements in *Madame Chrysanthème*.[15] The similarity, however, was in part the point, as Eaton placed the tropic Butterfly/Chrysanthème narrative on a different trajectory. Although the audience for all the three texts may not have been sensitive to the nuances separating them, we can see today that those differences carry meaning.[16] Long's narrative developed sympathy for the Japanese wife left behind in Loti's tale, and Eaton took the revision one step further by making her both sympathetic and powerful in her own right.

Instead of opening her novel, as Loti and Long did theirs, with two white sailors discussing the erotic possibilities of a temporary marriage to some young plaything from Japan, Eaton introduces us to Yuki before we know of Jack's existence. This initial centering of Yuki in our mind's eye establishes her as the center of the novel, even as the perspective gradually shifts to her American lover. She is positioned as an artist, one who mesmerizes teahouse audiences with her dancing, an actor who creates unique dances and negotiates contracts as a free agent. Well aware of her market value, both as a wife and a geisha dancer/singer, Yuki is hard-headed and realistic, unlike the hopelessly naive Cho-Cho-San who has little idea how to support herself beyond pitiful fantasies about the emperor's taking her under his wing or begging in the streets.

Japan is repositioned too. It is no longer first viewed as a port of entry for French or American sailors looking for exotic sex, but as a scene of magical transformation, "the witch-work of an Oriental Merlin" (100). The reader's eye is initially drawn to the curved bridges connecting the teahouse to the mainland, which metaphorically invites her to walk over a breast-shaped Japanese bridge to a new world of feminine enchantment. Rejecting the phallic Western bridge in favor of the female-gendered Japanese one will take the reader to a world where Japanese female and Western male can be blended in equality and harmony: "After crossing a bridge shaped thus [with a curve in the center], a straight bridge is forever an outrage to the eye and sense" (100).

The author focuses her readers on the teahouse bridge to emphasize the novel's bridging of West and East through its romantic presentation of mixed marriage and a bright, resourceful Eurasian heroine. Indeed, it is

---

[15] Van Rij describes the many ways Long's *Madame Butterfly* replicates the narrative elements of Loti's *Madame Chrysanthème* in *Madame Butterfly: Japonisme, Puccini, and the Search for the Real Cho-Cho-San* (2001).

[16] There were dramatic differences between the novel and stage versions of Long's and Eaton's stories as well. See Appendix for plot summaries of both plays.

Yuki's racially blended body that enacts scenes of such drama and beauty that her audiences are swept into new ways of feeling. Eaton encodes this bridging theme in several ways. As Yuko Matsukawa notes, Eaton's pen-name, Watanna, is composed of the Chinese ideograms "to cross" (*wata[ru]*) and "name" (*na*). Matsukawa concludes that this pun on her adopted last name foreshadows Eaton's career as "a tricksterlike figure who assumes multiple identities in order to straddle different spheres and disrupt the sense of reality and complacency of those worlds" (107).

The name Jack Bigelow, like Onoto Watanna, likewise straddles spheres. It places Eaton's character squarely within an Anglo-Saxon Protestant heritage and refers specifically to the Japanophile William Sturgis Bigelow, whose well-known books about Japan certainly contributed to both Eaton's and Long's store of knowledge about the country.[17] Both Jack Bigelow and William Sturgis Bigelow come from high-achieving, ambitious families, and both are graduates of Harvard.[18] Both also have relatively en-lightened views of the Japanese.

Another bridging figure in *A Japanese Nightingale* is Taro Burton, Yuki's Eurasian brother and protector. He is Jack's friend, a college chum at Harvard, who has bridged the cultural divide between Japan and America. He speaks English fluently, succeeds in the American educational system, and assumes a fatherly role with Yuki that is not patriarchal. Rather than welcome Jack's love, Yuki takes it for granted that their mar-riage will be temporary, in part because her brother has made her prom-ise not to marry a foreigner, and it is Taro who assumes a central place in Yuki's thoughts, though her American lover occupies her heart. Although his own parents' biracial marriage was stable, Taro believes it is the ex-ception that proves the rule, and he does not want to see his sister's life ru-ined by the temporary arrangements so ubiquitous in foreign ports of call. It is loyalty to her brother, not to her husband, that is uppermost in Yuki's thoughts as she saves money garnered from Jack to finance Taro's passage home.

Taro's bridging role is part of a larger reframing of the heroine's Japan-ese family in Eaton's novel. Unlike Loti's text, in which Chrysantheme's

---

[17] Eaton would later model another character on a noted Japanophile, William Elliott Griffis, in her novel *Tama* (1910).

[18] If Jack is the heir to a shipping fortune, William Sturgis Bigelow came from a more ac-ademic yet equally distinguished background: his grandfather was a physician and botanist, while his father was a surgeon and professor at Harvard Medical School. Lears notes that William Sturgis Bigelow's father was "almost a caricature of the self-reliant individual" (226).

Winnifred Eaton as Onoto Watanna. From
The Wooing of Wistaria by Onoto Watanna
(New York: Harper and Bros., 1902).

John Luther Long. H. B. Hansbury Studio. Reprinted by
permission of the Harry Ransom Humanities Research Center,
University of Texas–Austin.

David Belasco surrounded by sketches by Genjiro Yeto from the play The Darling of the Gods *(1903).* Harper's Weekly, *February 21, 1903.*

Scene from David Belasco's Madame Butterfly *(1900). Lieutenant Pinkerton (Frank Worthing) to Madame Butterfly (Blanche Bates): "Oh! Cho-Cho-San." From* Six Plays *by David Belasco (Boston: Little, Brown, and Co., 1928).*

Scenes from A Japanese Nightingale *(1903) with Margaret Illington as Yuki.* Harper's Weekly, *January 2, 1904.*

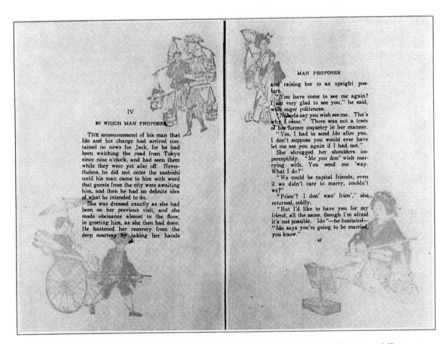

Page spread from A Japanese Nightingale *by Onoto Watanna (New York: Harper and Bros., 1901). Illustrated by Genjiro Yeto.*

family is narratively replaced by the couple's one-dimensional landlords, or Long's, where Cho-Cho-San's relatives are banished by Pinkerton and forever lost to her, Yuki's ties to her family remain strong. Her earnings as a geisha are turned over to her widowed Japanese mother, who depends on them for survival as well as for Taro's American education. It is Yuki's choice to keep Jack away from her family, and it is he who longs to know them, secretly following her at one point to her mother's doorstep. Yuki's family loyalty is the main threat to the marriage, not the American's desire to isolate his Japanese wife, as is the case in *Madame Butterfly*, nor has Yuki's family forced her into this marriage, as happens in both Loti's and Long's narratives.

Yuki's Japanese mother and Eurasian brother are humanized by Eaton, as is Yuki herself by her emotional connection to them. Cho-Cho-San's economic role vis-à-vis her family parallels that of Yuki—both characters support widows cast into desperate circumstances by their husbands' deaths. However, Eaton's narrative showcases the humanity of these characters, while Long's treats them as caricatures who exploit the young Cho-Cho-San. Yuki's mother, Omatsu, is given qualities admired and understood by an American audience at the turn of the century. She is overcome by grief when her son is felled by a terrible accident and her daughter disappears. She also mothers Jack when he is overcome by the tragic consequences of his actions and nurses him back to health. While she could easily blame him for the tragedy that befalls her children, she tenderly consoles him.

Taro too is imbued with positive qualities familiar to an American audience. He helps raise his little sister when they are young, treasures her as a precious soul mate, and angrily attacks his friend Jack for placing her in jeopardy. He is brotherly virtue incarnate, and his views of women are impeccably respectful, even feminist. It is Taro, in fact, who dies in the course of the narrative, a sacrificial figure emblematizing the dangers of mixed marriage, and in a sense he serves as the victim of Jack's irresponsibility, a stand-in for the iconic Butterfly. Although Eaton reinscribes the myth's portrayal of interracial love as damaging to a Japanese character, perhaps satisfying her audience's expectation that such a union inevitably produces victims, she showcases the vulnerability of an Asian man rather than a woman; Taro bridges gender as well as culture.[19]

---

[19] In her preceding novel, *Miss Numè of Japan* (1899), Eaton included another male sacrificial character, a Japanese educated at Harvard who falls in love with an American woman and kills himself when she spurns his marriage proposal.

This humanization extends to Yuki above all, whose emotional nature is multidimensional and instructive to the reader. Like Cho-Cho-San, Yuki shares with her literary forerunner a vivid imagination, a deep capacity for romantic love, and tremendous loyalty. Unlike Long's tragic geisha, however, Yuki's feelings are not focused entirely on her lover but flow from a complex mixture of identification with the natural world, an acute sense of her outcast status, and overarching concern for her family's well-being. Even before she meets Jack, her signature "storm dance" announces the inner turmoil she experiences as an outsider in her own land, but it is a trial she turns into art. Nature furnishes Yuki with an artistic palette, and it also gives her a way to locate herself in a society that marginalizes her. She transcends the social codes that label her an outcast, simultaneously creating sympathy in her audience (both within and outside of the text) and leading it into a landscape more beautiful and hospitable than that created by the laws of men.

While both Long and Eaton revise myths of the inscrutable, placid, mysterious Asian devoid of emotion, Eaton's text places the transformative power of love in the character of Yuki, whose charm stems from her connection to the natural world and her uniqueness. Cho-Cho-San, in contrast, is the one who is transformed by the refinement of romantic feeling and emotional spontaneity brought to her by Pinkerton. It is the American who is awakened in *A Japanese Nightingale* by Yuki's vitality, whereas the childlike, naive Butterfly is brought to life by Pinkerton, only to be killed off by his neglect.

There are many such reversals in *Nightingale*, all of which empower and humanize Yuki. In *Madame Butterfly*, Cho-Cho-San, practically imprisoned in the pseudo-Japanese home Pinkerton provides her, longs to move to the United States with him and fantasizes about living under Christian marriage laws and even about conversion. The tragic dénouement of the story occurs when Cho-Cho-San sights Pinkerton's ship but soon realizes she has an American rival who will destroy her dream of reunion and family harmony. It is the rival, Pinkerton's wife, Adelaide, whom we last see in the narrative, arriving at Cho-Cho-San's empty house to take her baby away.[20] In contrast, Yuki dismisses Christianity, works to bring her brother *back* from the United States, and declares her intention never to leave her homeland with her first words in the text: "I stay ad Japan" (104). It is she who disappears and lives on an American

---

[20] In the play and opera, it is Pinkerton who arrives at the abandoned love nest wherein his self-sacrificing Japanese wife lies mortally wounded.

ship touring Asia for two years while Jack searches futilely for her; the American lover is rooted in Japan and the geisha sails the high seas. The climax of *Nightingale* turns *Butterfly*'s dénouement inside out. Jack is just about to leave Tokyo when word reaches him that Yuki has been spotted. He returns to their conjugal home, as Pinkerton does in the play, and Adelaide does in Long's story, but instead of finding a dying or vanished geisha, he encounters a very alive Yuki in her bedroom. They joyfully reunite amid the cherry blossoms of spring, a season that was to have signaled Pinkerton's return.

Jack's unswerving loyalty and compelling attraction to Yuki are important elements in *A Japanese Nightingale,* which Eaton deliberately fashioned, we believe, as a counter-narrative to the Butterfly myth. She was well aware of the implicit racism underlying the notion that American sailors used Japanese women as exotic, erotic playthings, only to abandon them for the more acceptable women at home. Indeed, she spoke out against such liaisons when *A Japanese Nightingale* opened on Broadway: "I do not think international marriages are wise, as a rule. Certainly, they are unfortunate for the Japanese woman . . . for the European or American does not consider such a marriage binding."[21]

She also could not help but notice the Caucasian beauty standards of her day. Despite American fascination with delicate Japanese femininity, for example, it was white women dressed in kimonos and surrounded by Japanese artifacts who served as portraiture subjects for Western painters in the *Japonisme* era.[22] Her own play featured an all-white cast, with Margaret Illington playing the role of Yuki, and the 5'7" white actress Blanche Bates played Cho-Cho-San in Belasco's *Madame Butterfly*, as well as the Japanese heroine of Belasco's *The Darling of the Gods* in 1903. Puccini similarly cast Italian sopranos in his 1904 opera, and it was a white American soprano, Geraldine Farrar, who built her career on singing the part when the opera debuted at New York City's Metropolitan Opera House in 1907.[23]

Although she surely must have been struck by the irony of white

---

[21] "Jap Artist Sees 'A Japanese Nightingale.'"

[22] John Singer Sargent, James Whistler, William Merritt Chase, and Robert Henri were among the many such painters who featured white models in kimonos. Only Japanese artists painted the famous scenes of geisha in authentic Japanese settings.

[23] It was not until 1914 that a Japanese woman, Miura Tamaki (1884–1946), was cast as Cho-Cho-San in Puccini's opera. Mari Yoshihara discusses the phenomenon of white women cross-dressing as Japanese at this time in "In Search of Mrs. Pinkerton," a chapter in her forthcoming book.

actresses impersonating Japanese women when she herself was masquerading as a Japanese noblewoman to hide her Chinese ethnicity, Eaton never mentioned the racial politics of such cross-dressing publicly. Instead, she focused her attention on valorizing Asian beauty: "Most men admire Miss Chrysanthemum, and naval officers of all countries—even outside of comic opera—adore her, especially Englishmen and Americans. Yes, and when they have their own beautiful women from which to draw comparisons."[24] The framing of Yuki as an irresistible beauty whose Eurasian features are regarded as ugly in her native country addresses this privileging of white beauty standards. Eaton displaces the American rival who bests Cho-Cho-San in *Madame Butterfly* and creates instead a faux rival in Jack's sister, whose photograph arouses Yuki's jealousy (needlessly, as she quickly finds out). In addition, Pinkerton's wife is replaced by the theatrical agent's young American wife, who protects Yuki and brings her back to Japan. In contrast to Adelaide, who comes to Japan to take away Cho-Cho-San's child—claiming it for herself—the young American wife in *Nightingale* comes expressly to hasten the lovers' happy reunion.

Eaton walked a difficult tightrope in crafting *A Japanese Nightingale*'s widened cultural parameters, for the nativism of her era ran broad and deep. She had no Asian literary role models beyond the pulp fiction perpetuating flawed to ugly stereotypes or the tragic figure of her older sister, whose writing she admired but who published only one book (*Mrs. Spring Fragrance and Other Stories*, 1912), remained single, and languished in ill health until her death in 1914 at the age of forty-nine.[25] *Nightingale*'s exaggerated dialect, melodramatic plot, shallow characterization, and purple prose are aesthetic flaws that mar its reading for us today, but they need to be understood as part of the price Eaton paid to get her novel into print. As a young Chinese-North American from a poor family, a working woman who did not have the financial resources that might have allowed her more artistic freedom or time to revise and polish her fiction, Eaton's decisions about how to write would always be heavily influenced by her dependence on the popular market.

Eaton also wished to change the image of Asian people, particularly women, in American culture, and the commercial market was the ground on which she chose to fight this battle. As she wrote of her goals in her 1915 autobiography *Me*, "[I had] dreams of the fame and fortune that not

---

[24] "Jap Artist Sees 'A Japanese Nightingale.'"

[25] Winnifred Eaton married twice, had four children, and died in 1954 when she was seventy-eight. She published fourteen novels in book form and an autobiography.

alone should lift me up, but all my people" (194). That she meant to challenge the Orientalist racism of her era is clear from this and other statements, such as the essay she published in 1907 attacking anti-Japanese sentiment increasingly evident in the American press:

> To speak of the Oriental nations as inferior is to make an ignorant and stupid statement. . . . Are we no better than in the time when the white-skinned Spaniards came all conquering to exterminate the darker-hued man of the New World? Do the Western nations, indeed, cherish the childish delusion that a race as proud and intelligent as the Japanese or Chinese could be likewise subjected?[26]

As a commercial writer, Winnifred Eaton chose not to violate the literary formulas regarding race, gender, and romance that fueled American society's sense of its superiority to Asia, but she did revise them to include a Eurasian female voice of considerable power in this, her most successful novel. Though she, like her heroine, survived by imitating something she was not, Eaton created a wedge that made possible her presence as an artist with a new vision. She made a cultural space for the talented, lovable, admirable Asian woman with a dual heritage, for the outsider who had something of value to offer those inhabiting the center. If that space seems obvious to us today, if it seems inadequate indeed for our current vision, *A Japanese Nightingale* is no less significant as an important initial step toward the self-consciously and even defiantly Asian American literature of our current multicultural environment.

---

[26] "The Japanese in America," *The Eclectic Magazine* 148 (February 1907): 100–104.

Note on the Texts

THIS edition is based on the first book publication of *Madame Butterfly* (Century, 1898), with illustrations from the first magazine publication (*The Century Illustrated Magazine,* January 1898; frontispiece) and the "Japanese edition" published in 1903 (Century; in-text illustrations); and the first edition of *A Japanese Nightingale* (Harper and Bros., 1901). The texts have been edited to conform to modern spelling and usage, but remain otherwise as they first appeared.

Long and Eaton most likely developed their form of "Japanese American dialect" from the popular stage, where caricatures of Japanese (as well as other ethnic minorities) were immensely popular.[1] Nevertheless, present-day readers may feel that the speech of Cho-Cho-San and Yuki are often unnecessarily exaggerated and distorted. Spellings such as "loog" for "look," "lig" for "like," and "aexcep'" for "except" violate spelling conventions far out of proportion to the actual difference in pronunciation that would occur when the words are spoken aloud. George Krapp describes this technique of rendering "non-standard" speech as "eye dialect": written language in which "the convention violated is one of the eyes, not of the ear" (228). Examples more familiar to modern readers would be the spelling of "gonna" for "going to," and "wuz" for "was." Krapp and others have noted that the primary effect of eye dialect is not the achievement of exact verisimilitude, but the assertion of difference — a difference that often asserts "a sympathetic sense of superiority between the author and reader as contrasted with the humble speaker of dialect" (228). The appropriation of dialect by ethnic writers such as Eaton (as well as contemporaries such as Charles Chesnutt and Paul Laurence Dunbar, as well as many writers in the twentieth century), of course, challenges and complicates this conventional relationship.

A glossary that includes Japanese and dialect words used frequently in these texts has been provided at the end of the volume. The most common

---

[1] See Jones for an analysis of dialect fiction in the nineteenth and early twentieth centuries, and Moy, chaps. 3 and 4, for examples of Chinese American dialect used on the American stage and in vaudeville.

orthographic distortions of standard English spellings are the substitution of d's for t's and th's ("nod" for "not," "nodder" for "another," "ride" for "right") and g's for k's ("lige" or "lig" for "like"). Other aspects of the dialect that may cause confusion for modern readers include subject-verb disagreement, incorrectly conjugated verbs ("he saying"), misused and omitted prepositions, and manufactured words ("I got not ancestors whichever"). Fortunately, these conventions remain consistent through both texts.

Madame Butterfly

·

John Luther Long

"She had a sword in her lap as she sat down." From Madame Butterfly *by John Luther Long (New York: Century, 1903). Illustrated by C. Yarnall Abbott.*

CONTENTS

I.

Sayre's Prescription

SAYRE had counseled him on the voyage out (for he had repined cease-lessly at what he called their banishment to the Asiatic station) to wait till they arrived. *He* had never regarded service in Japanese waters as ban-ishment, he said, and he had been out twice before.

Pinkerton had just come from the Mediterranean.

"For lack of other amusement," continued Sayre, with a laugh, "you might get yourself married and—"

Pinkerton arrested him with a savage snort.

"You are usually merely frivolous, Sayre; but to-day you are silly."

Without manifest offense, Sayre went on:

"When I was out here in 1890—"

"The story of the Pink Geisha?"[1]

"Well—yes," admitted Sayre, patiently.

"Excuse me, then, till you are through." He turned to go below.

"Heard it, have you?"

"A thousand times from you and others."

Sayre laughed good-naturedly at the gallant exaggeration, and passed Pinkerton his cigarette-case.

"Ah—ever heard who the man was?"

"No." He lighted his cigarette. "That has been your own little mys-tery—apparently."

"Apparently?"

---

[1] Two months after the sensational 1898 publication of "Madame Butterfly" in *The Century*, Long proposed a sequel along the lines of the "Pink Geisha" story alluded to here. In a letter to R. W. Gilder, the editor, he described a story in which Sayre marries (unknowingly) a samurai's wife, a famous dancer known as "The Pink Geisha," because of a pink mask she wears in performances. When he discovers the truth, Sayre leaves Japan in a fit of anger, only to return for his lost love when he discovers her husband is an invalid and has pushed her into the marriage so he could pay off a debt to Sayre. He returns to find that she and the samurai have committed suicide together because of the shame incurred from the affair. Gilder replied tersely, "I can see how the enclosed 'lay out' attracts you—But I am sorry—for it is questionable whether Jap. [sic] ideas can be instilled into American minds."

"Yes; we all knew it was yourself."

"It wasn't," said Sayre, steadily. It was my brother." He looked away.

"Oh!"

"He's dead."

"Beg pardon. You never told us that."

"He went back; couldn't find her."

"And you advise me also to become a subject for remorse? That's good of you."

"It is not quite the same thing. There is no danger of you losing your head for—" he glanced uncertainly at Pinkerton, then ended lamely— "anyone. The danger would probably be entirely with—the other person."

"Thanks," laughed Pinkerton, "that's more comforting."

"And yet," mused Sayre, "you are hard to comfort—humanly speaking." Pinkerton smiled at this naive but quite exact characterization of himself.

"You are," continued Sayre, hesitating for the right word— "impervious."

"Exactly," laughed Pinkerton. "I *don't* see much danger to myself in your prescription. You have put it in rather an attractive light. The idea cannot be entirely disreputable if your brother Jack used it. We lower-class[2] fellows used to call him Agamemnon,[3] you remember."

"It is not my prescription," said Sayre, briefly, leaving the deck.

---

[2] In a lower college class; lower classmen; that is, freshmen or sophomores as opposed to juniors and seniors.

[3] Pinkerton may be referring to Agamemnon's theft of Briseis from Achilles, which was the catalyst for a crisis in the Greek camp in the Trojan War, or his later receipt of Cassandra as concubine—implying that Sayre's brother Jack was a roué. Or he might be referring to Agamemnon's cuckolding and murder at the hands of Clytemnestra.

II.

Mr. B. F. Pikkerton—and His Way

BUT Pinkerton not only got himself married; he provided himself with an establishment—creating his ménage in quite his own way and entirely for his own comfort.

With the aid of a marriage-broker, he found both a wife and a house in which to keep her. This he leased for nine hundred and ninety-nine years. Not, he explained to his wife later, that he could hope for the felicity of residing there with her so long, but because, being a mere "barbarian,"[4] he could not make other legal terms. He did not mention that the lease was determinable, nevertheless, at the end of any month, by the mere neglect to pay the rent. Details were distasteful to Pinkerton; besides, she would probably not appreciate the humor of this.

Some clever Japanese artisans then made the paper walls of the pretty house eye-proof, and, with their own adaptations of American hardware, the openings cunningly lockable. The rest was Japanese.

Madame Butterfly laughed, and asked him why he had gone to all that trouble—in Japan!

"To keep out those who are out, and in those who are in," he replied, with an amorous threat in her direction.

She was greatly pleased with it all, though, and went about jingling her new keys and her new authority like toys,—she had only one small maid to command,—until she learned that among others to be excluded were her own relatives.

There had been what her husband called an appalling horde of these at the wedding (they had come with lanterns and banners and disturbing evidences of good will), and he asked her, when she questioned him, whether she did not think they would be a trifle wearisome.

"*You* thing so?" she asked in turn.

"Emphatically," said her husband.

She grew pale; she had not expected quite such an answer. A Japanese would have said no, but would have left an interrogation in one's mind.

---

[4] Japanese term (translated) for a Westerner, primarily used in the nineteenth century.

He laughed consolingly.

"Well, Ane-San" (which meant only "elder sister": there are no terms of endearment in the Japanese language), "you will have to get along without ancestors. Think of the many people who would like to do that, and be comforted."

"Who?" She had never heard of such a thing.

"People, for instance, whose ancestors have perished on the gallows, or, in America, have practiced trades."[5]

She did not understand, as often she did not, and he went on:

"I shall have to serve in the capacity of ancestors,—let us say ancestors-at-large,—and the real ones will have to go—or rather not come."

Again he had the joke to himself; his wife had gone away to cry.

At first she decided to run away from him. But this, she reflected, would not probably please her relatives, since they had unanimously agreed upon the marriage for her. Besides, she preferred to remain. She had acquired a strange liking for Pinkerton and her new way of life. Finally she undertook a weak remonstrance—a very strong one, in fact, for a Japanese wife; but Pinkerton encouraged her pretty domestic autonomy. Her airs of authority were charming. And they grew more and more so.

"Mr. B. F. Pikkerton,"—it was this, among other things, he had taught her to call him,—"I lig if you permit my august ancestors visit me. I lig ver' *moach* if you *please* permit that unto me."

Her hair had been newly dressed for the occasion, and she had stuck a poppy in it. Besides, she put her hand on his arm (a brave thing for her to do), and smiled wistfully up at him. And when you know what Cho-Cho-San's smile was like,[6]—and her hand—and its touch,—you will wonder how Pinkerton resisted her. However, he only laughed at her,—good-naturedly always,—and said no.

"We can't adopt a whole regiment of back numbers,[7] you know. You are back number enough for me."

And though he kissed her, she went away and cried again; and Japanese girls do not often cry.

He could not understand how important this concession was to her. It must be confessed that he did not try to understand. Sayre, with a little partisanship, explained to him that in Japan filial affection is the para-

---

[5] That is, descendents of criminals and the artisanal (as opposed to land-owning) class.

[6] An affectionate nickname in Japanese is constructed this way by doubling the short form of the first name and adding "san" or "chan."

[7] "Back number," back issue of a magazine.

mount motive, and that these "ancestors," living and dead, were his wife's sole link to such eternal life as she hoped for. He trusted that Pinkerton would not forget this.

He would provide her a new motive, then, Pinkerton said,—perhaps meaning himself,—and a new religion if she *must* have one—himself, again. So when she, at his motion, diffidently undertook to clothe the phantoms which made up her "religion," Pinkerton expounded what he called the easier Western plan of salvation—seriously, too, considering that all his communications to her were touched with whimsy. This was inevitable—to Pinkerton. After all, she *was* quite an impossible little thing, outside of lacquer and paint. But he struck deeper than he knew; for she went secretly to the church of the missionary who served on the opposite hill, and heard the same thing, and learned, moreover, that she might adopt this new religion at any time she chose—even the eleventh hour.

She went out joyously; not to adopt his religion, it is true, but to hold it in reserve if her relatives should remain obdurate. Pinkerton, to his relief, heard no more of it.

III.

A Moon-Goddess Truly

overstating the "non Christian aspect" from page 1 continues...

Bᴜᴛ his wife's family (the word has a more important application there than here) held a solemn conference, and, as the result of it, certain of them waited upon Lieutenant Pinkerton, and, with elaborate politeness, intimated that his course had theretofore been quite unknown in Japan. This was their oblique way of saying that it was unsatisfactory. They pointed out with patient gravity that he would thus limit his wife's opportunities of reappearing on earth in a higher form of life.

Buddhist?

Pinkerton smilingly remarked that he was not sure that it would be best for his wife to reappear on earth in a higher form. She would probably accomplish mischief enough in this very charming one—as she was in fact doing.

"Do you know," he continued to the spokesman, "that you look exactly like a lacquered tragedy mask I have hanging over my desk?"

One must have seen one of these masks to appreciate this.

But they all laughed good-naturedly, as their host had designed, and quite forgot their errand. And Pinkerton labored that they should remember it no more. This was quite Japanese. In the politest way possible he made them drink his liquors and smoke his tobacco (in the generous Western fashion), either of which operations was certain to make a Japanese very ill. This was thoroughly like Pinkerton.

Cho Cho "san"? Korean - Japanese etc.?

They protested a deal of friendship for Pinkerton that night; but at the final conference, where Cho-Cho-San was solemnly disowned, none were more gloomily unfriendly than they who had eaten and drunk with him.

"I did the very best I could for you, little moon-goddess," said Pinkerton to his wife; "but they were proof against my best wine and tobacco."

She bent her head in reflection a moment.

"Ah, you mean—I begin learn you, Mr. B. F. Pikkerton! You mean they *not* proof. Aha!"

And Pinkerton delightedly embraced her.

"You are no longer a back number," he said.

"Aha! Tha' 's what *I* thing. Now I bed you I know what *is* that bag nomber!"

"Well?"

"People lig I *was*."

"Exactly."

"But not people lig I *am*?"

"No; you are up-to-date."

"I egspeg I ought be sawry?" She sighed hypocritically.

"Exactly why, my moon-maid?"

"Account they outcasting me. Aeverybody thing me mos' bes' wicked in all Japan. Nobody speak to me no more—they all outcast me *aex*cep' jus' you; tha' 's why I ought be sawry."

She burst into a reckless laugh, and threw herself like a child upon him. "But tha' 's ezag' why I am *not*! Wha' 's use lie? It is not inside me— that sawry. Me? I'm mos' bes' happy female woman in Japan—mebby in that whole worl'. What you thing?"

He said honestly that he thought she was, and he took honest credit for it.

IV.

Trouble—Meaning Joy

AND after his going, in the whimsical delight they had practiced together, she named the baby, when it came, Trouble. Every Japanese baby begins with a temporary name; it may be anything, almost, for the little time. She was quite sure he would like the way she had named him Trouble—meaning joy. That was his own oblique way. As for his permanent name,—he might have several others before,—that was for him to choose when he returned. And this event was to happen, according to his own words, when the robins nested again.

And spring and the robins had come.

All this to explain why Madame Butterfly and her baby were reclining on the immaculate mats in attitudes of artistic abandon, instead of keeping an august state, as all other Japanese mothers and babes were at this moment doing. American women, we are told, assume more fearless attitudes in the security of their boudoirs than elsewhere. Japanese women, never. Their conduct is eternally the same. It must be as if someone were looking on—always. There is no privacy for them short of the grave. They have no secure boudoirs.

But Madame Butterfly (through the courtesy of her American husband) had both these. It will therefore be argued, perhaps, that she is not a typical Japanese woman. But it is only Lieutenant Pinkerton's views about which we are presently concerned. He called her an American refinement of a Japanese product, an American improvement on a Japanese invention, and so on. And since he knew her best, his words concerning her should have a certain ex-cathedra authority. I know no more.

And she and the maid, and the baby too, were discussing precisely the matters which have interested us hitherto—Pinkerton, his baby, his imminent return, etc.

Cho-Cho-San, with a deft jerk that was also a caress, brought the baby into her lap as she sat suddenly up.

"Ah, *you*—you think he is just like any other baby. But—he is a mira-

"But—he is a miracle! Yes!" From Madame Butterfly by John Luther Long (New York: Century, 1903). Illustrated by C. Yarnall Abbott.

cle! Yes!" she insisted belligerently. "The Sun-Goddess sent him straight from the Bridge of Heaven! Because of those prayers so early—oh, so *very* early in the morning. Oh, that is the time to pray!" She turned the baby violently so that she might see his eyes. "Now did anyone *ever* hear of a Japanese baby with purple eyes?"

She held him over against the dwarfed wisteria which grew in a flat bronze koro at the tokonoma, full of purple blossoms. She addressed the maid Suzuki, who stood by, happy as herself, apparently aware that this subject must always be discussed vehemently.

"As purple as that! Answer me, thou giggler; is it not so? Speak! I *will* have an answer!"

Then the maid laughed out a joyous no. If she cherished the Eastern reservations concerning blue eyes and pink cheeks, it was a less heinous offense to lie about it a little than to assert it impolitely. Besides, neither she nor anyone else could resist the spirits of her pretty mistress. And these spirits had grown joyously riotous since her marriage and its unfettering.

"Nor yet so bald of his head? Say so! Quickly!" she insisted, with the manner of Pinkerton—such is example!

The maid also agreed to this.

And then Cho-Cho-San flung the kicking youngster high above her, turned abandonedly over on her back (in charming, if forbidden, postures),[8] and juggled with him there.

"But ah! you *will* have hair, will you not?—as long and glittering as that of the American women. I will not endure thee else." She became speciously savage. "Speak, thou beggar, speak!"

"Goo-goo," said the baby, endeavoring diligently to obey.

She shook him threateningly.

"Ah-h-h! You making that non-*senze* with your parent? Now what *is* that you speaking with me? Jap'nese? If it is, I—" She threatened him direly. But he had evidently already learned to understand her; he gurgled again. "Listen! *No* one shall speak anything but United States' languages in these house! *Now!* What you thing? You go'n' go right outside shoji firs' thing you do that!" She resumed her own English more ostentatiously,—she forgot it herself sometimes,—and pretended to pitch the baby through the fragile paper wall.

"Also, tha' 's one thing *aevery*body got recomleck—account it is his house, his wife, his bebby, his maiden, his moaney—oh,—*aevery*thing is

---

[8] Cho-Cho-San's behavior is quite immodest for a Japanese woman, especially of this period.

his! An' he say, those time he go'n' 'way, that *aex*cep' we all talking those United States' languages when he come, he go'n' bounce us all. *Well!* I don' git myself bounce, Mr. Trouble! An' you got loog out you don', aha! Sa-*ay*, me? I thing if we doing all those thing he as' us, he go'n' take us at those United States America, an' live in his castle. Then he never *kin* bounce us, aha!"

V.

A Song of Sorrow—and Death—and Heaven

A bird flew to the vine in the little porch.

"Ah, Suzuki!"

But the maid had withdrawn. She clapped her hands violently for her to return.

"Now why *do* you go 'way when"—her momentary anger fled, and she laughed—"when birds flying to the wisteria? Go quickly, little maiden, and see if he is a robin, and if he has completed his nest—quickly."

The maid returned, and said that he was indeed a robin, but that he had no nest there as yet.

"Oh, *how* he is slow! Suzuki, let us fine 'nother robin, one that is more industrious—an' domes-tic, aha, ha, ha!"

"They are all alike," said the girl, cynically.

"They—*not!* Say so!"

Suzuki giggled affirmatively. When her mistress took so violently to English she preferred to express herself in this truly Japanese fashion.

"Inform me, if you please, how much nearer beggary we are to-day than yesterday, Suzuki." The girl had exact information for her on this subject. She said they had just seventeen yen, fifty-four sen, two rin.[9]

"Alas—alas! *How* we have waste his beau-tiful moaneys! Tha' 's shame. *But* he will not permit that we starve—account he know we have no one *ae*xcep' him. We all outcasted. Now loog *how* that is bad! *So* jus' when it is all gone he will come with more—lig the stories of ole Kaz-abu. *Oh!* lig story of Uncombed Ronin, who make a large oath that he go'n' be huge foo-el if he dress his hair until his lord arrive back from the banishment. *Lo!* when they cutting his hade off him, account he don' comb his hair, his lord arrive back, an' say, 'What they doing with him?'—an' reward him great deal, account he constant ontil he 'mos' dead. *So,* jus' when we go'n' out on the street,—mebby to fine him,—you with Trouble on your back, me with my samisen, standing up be-

---

[9] They have about $170 left.

fore all the people, singing funeral songs, with faces, oh, 'bout 'mos' so long,"—she illustrated liberally,—"sad garments, hair all ruffled—so, dancing liddle—so,"—she indicated how she should dance,—"an' saying out ver' loud, 'O ye people! Listen, for the loave of all the eight hundred thousan' gods and goddesses! Behole, we, a poor widow, an' a bebby what got purple eyes, which had one hosban', which gone off at United States America, to naever return no more— *naever!* Aexcep' you have seen him? No? See! This what I thing. Oh, how that is mos' tarrible! We giving up all our august ancestors, an' gods, an' people, an' country,—oh, *aeverything*,—jus' for him, an' now he don' naever come no more! Oh, *how* that is sad! Is it not? Also, he don' even divorce us, so that we kin marry with 'nother mans an' git some food. *He?* He don' even *thing* 'bout it! Not liddle bit! He forgitting us—alas! *But* we got keep his house nine hundred an' ninety-nine year! Now thing 'bout *that!* An' we go'n' starve before, *aex*cep' you giving us—ah-ah-*ah!* jus' one sen! two sen! mebby fi' sen! Oh, for the loave of sorrow, for the loave of constancy, for the loave of death, jus'—one—sen! Will you please pity us? In the name of the merciful Kwannon we beg. Loog! To move your hearts in the inside you, we go'n' sing you a song of sorrow—an' death—an' heaven."

She had acted it all with superb spirit, and now she snatched up her samisen, and dramatized this also; and so sure was she of life and happiness that this is the song of sorrow and death she sang:

"Hikari nodokeki haru no nobe,
Niwo sakura-no-hana sakari,
Mure kuru hito no tanoshiki ni,
Shibashi uki yo ya wasururan."

"Sunshine on a quiet plain in spring,
The perfume of the blooming cherry-blossoms,
The joy of the gathering crowd,
Filled with love, forget the care of life."

And then, as always, abandonment and laughter.
"Aha, ha, ha! Aha, ha, ha! What you thing, liddle maiden? Tha' 's good song 'bout sorrow, an' death, an' heaven? Aha, ha, ha! What—you—thing? Speak! Say so!"
She tossed the samisen to its place, and sprang savagely at the maid.

"If that Mr. B. F. Pikkerton see us doing lig those—" ventured the maid, in the humor of her mistress.

"O-o-o! You see his eye flame an' scorch lig lightening! O-o-o! He snatch us away to the house—so—so—*so!*"

The baby was the unfortunate subject for the illustration of this. He began to whimper.

"Rog-a-by, bebby, off in Japan,
You jus' a picture off of a fan."—

[handwritten annotations: didn't he originate there? drunk? Malnourishment? drugs or mental illness author of character?]

This was from Pinkerton. She had been the baby then.

"Ah, liddle beggar, he di'n' know he go'n' make those poetries for you! He don' suspect of you whichever. *Well!* I bed you we go'n' have some fun when he *do.* Oh, Suzuki! Some day, when the emperor go abroad, we will show him. You got say these way"—she changed her voice to what she fancied an impressive male basso: "'Behole, Heaven-Descended-Ruler-Everlasting-Great-Japan, the first of your subjecks taken his eye out those ver' blue heaven whence you are descend!' Hence the emperor loog on him; then he *stop* an' loog; he kin naever git enough loogs. Then he make Trouble a large prince! An' me? He jus' say onto me: 'Continue that you bring out such sons.' Aha, ha, ha! What you thing?"

The maid was frankly skeptical.

"At least you kin do lig the old nakodo wish you—for you are most beautiful."[10]

[handwritten annotations: Psychosis? 是三佳× not even an ape would do th...]

Cho-Cho-San dropped the baby with a reckless thud, and sprang at her again. She gripped her throat viciously, then flung her, laughing, aside.

"Speak concerning marriage once more, an' you die. An' tha' 's 'nother thing. You got know at his United States America, if one is marry one got stay marry—oh, for aever an' aever! *Yaes!* Nob'y cannot git himself divorce, *aex*cep' in a large courthouse an' jail. Tha' 's way with he—that Mr. B. F. Pikkerton—an' me—that Mrs. B. F. Pikkerton. If he aever go'n' divorce me, he got take me at those large jail at that United States America. Tha' 's lot of trouble; hence he rather stay marry with me. Also, he *lig* be marry with me. Now loog! He leave me a'mos' largest lot money in Japan; he give me his house for live inside for nine hundred an' ninety-nine year. I cannot go home at my grandmother, account he make them

---

[10] Suzuki is referring to the matchmaker who arranged Cho-Cho-San's marriage with Pinkerton, and suggests that she avail herself of his services again since Pinkerton has apparently abandoned her.

outcast me. Sa-*ay*, you liddle foolish! He coming when the robins nest again. Aha! What you thing? Say so!"

The maid should have been excused for not being always as <u>recklessly jubilant</u> as her mistress; but she never was. And now, when she chose silence rather than speech (which was both more prudent and more polite), she took it very ill.

VI.

Divine Foolery

I<small>F</small> Pinkerton had told her to go home, even though she had no home to go to, she would have been divorced without more ado. Perhaps she was logical (for she reasoned as he had taught her—she had never reasoned before) in considering that as he had distinctly told her not to do so, it was an additional surety for his return.

Cho-Cho-San again took up the happier side of the matter. The baby was asleep.

"An' also, what you thing we bedder doing when he come?"

She was less forcible now, because less certain. This required planning to get the utmost felicity out of it—what she always strove for.

"Me?—I thing I—dun*no,*" the maid confessed diplomatically.

"Aha, ha, ha! You dun*no*? Of course you dunno whichever! Well—I go'n' tell you." The plan had been born and matured that instant in her active little brain. "Jus' recomleck 't is a secret among you an' me. We don' tell that Mr. Trouble. Hoash! He don' kin keep no secret. *Well,* listen! We go'n' watch with that spying-glass till his ship git in. Then we go'n' put cherry-blossoms aeverywhere; an' if 't is night, we go'n' hang up 'bout 'mos' one thousan' lanterns—'bout 'mos' one thousan'! Then we—*wait.* Jus' when we see him coming up that hill—so—so—so—*so,*"—she lifted her kimono, and strode masculinely about the apartment,—"then! We hide behine the shoji, where there are holes to peep." She glanced about to find them. "Alas! they all mended shut! *But*"—she savagely ran her finger through the paper—"we soon make some, aha, ha, ha! So!" She made another for the maid. They illustrated this phase of her mood with their eyes at the holes. "Then we lie quiet lig mice, an' make believe we gone 'way. Better n' we leave liddle note: 'Gone 'way foraever. Sayonara, Butterfly'? No; tha' 's too long for him. He git angery those ways on the first word, an' say those remark 'bout debbil, an' hell, an' all kind loud languages. Tha' 's time, before he gitting *too* angery, to rush out, an' jump all roun' his neck, aha!" This was also illustrated.

But, alas! the maid was too realistic.

"Sa-*ay*! not *you*—jump roun' his neck—jus' *me.*"

Cho-Cho-San paused ecstatically. But the maid would not have it so. She had seen them practice such divine foolery,—very like two reckless children,—but never had she seen anything with such dramatic promise as this.

"Oh! an' what he say *then*," she begged, with wild interest, "an' what he *do*?"

Madame Butterfly was reenergized by the maid's applause.

"Ah-h-h!" she sighed. "He don' *say*—jus' he *kiss* us, oh, 'bout three— seven—ten—a thousan' time! An' amberace us two thousan' time 'bout 'mos'—tha' 's what he *do*—till we got make him stop, aha, ha, ha! account he might—might—*kill* us! Tha' 's *ver*' bad to be kill kissing."

Her extravagant mood infected the maid. She had long ago begun to wonder whether, after all, this American passion of affection was altogether despicable. She remembered that her mistress had begun by regarding it thus; yet now she was the most daringly happy woman in Japan.

"Say more," the maid pleaded.

Cho-Cho-San had a fine fancy, and the nesting of the robins could not, at the longest, be much longer delayed now; she let it riot.[11]

"Well,"—she was making it up as she went,—"when tha' 's all done, he loog roun' those ways lig he doing 'mos' always, an' he see sump'n', an' he say: 'Oh, 'el-*lo*—'el-lo! Where you got that chile?' I say: 'Ah—oh—*ah*! I thing mebby you lig own one, an' I buy 'm of a man what di'n' wan' no bebby with those purple eye an' bald hairs.' And he as' me, 'What you pay?' Americans always as' what you pay. I say: 'Oh, lemme see. I thing, two yen an' two sen. Tha' 's too moach for bald bebby? What you thing?' But tha' 's a time he saying: 'I bed you tha' 's a liar; an' you fooling among me.' Then he gitting angery, an' I hurry an' say, one las' time, 'Tha' 's right. I tole you liddle lie for a *fun*. I di'n' pay *naw*thing for him, *aex*cep'— sa-*ay*!—' Then I whisper a thing inside his ear,—jus' a liddle thing,—an' he *see*! Aha, ha, ha! Then he say once more, las' time,—ah, what you thing, Suzuki?"

But the girl would not diminish her pleasure by guessing.

"'*God*amighty!' Aha, ha, ha!"

"Tha' 's all things you know?" questioned the maid, reproachfully, "an' all things you do?"

She had a right to feel that she had been defrauded out of a proper dénouement.

---

[11] That is, she let her imagination run wild.

"Ah-h-h-h! What would you have that is more? Jus' joy an' glory foraevermore! Tha' 's 'nough. What you thing? You know that song?

> "'T is life when we meet,
> 'T is death when we part."

Her mistress had grown plaintive in those two lines.

"I hear him sing that," murmured the maid, comfortingly.

Her spirits vaulted up again.

"But ah! You aever hear him sing—?"

She snatched up the samisen again, and to its accompaniment sang, in the pretty jargon he had taught her (making it as grotesque as possible, the more to amuse him):

> "I call her the belle of Japan—of Japan;
> Her name it is O Cho-Cho-San—Cho-Cho-San;
> Such tenderness lies in her soft almond eyes,
> I tell you she's just ichi ban."

"Tha' 's *me*—aha, ha, ha! Sa-*ay*—you thing he aever going away again when he got that liddle chile, an' the samisen, an' the songs, an' all the joy, an'—an' *me*?" And another richly joyous laugh.

"Oh, you an' the samisen an' joy—poof!" said the maid. "But the chile—tha' 's 'nother kind thing. *Aexcep' he* grow up, an' go 'way after his father?"

She was odiously unsatisfied. She would leave nothing to fate—to heaven—Shaka. But out of her joyous future her mistress satisfied even this grisly doubt.

"Ah-h-h! *But* we go'n' have *more*—lig steps of a ladder, up, up, up! An' all purple eyes—oh, aevery one! An' all males! Then, if one go 'way, we got 'nother an' 'nother an' 'nother. Then, how *kin* he, that Mr. B. F. Pikkerton, aever go 'way? Aha!"

"Yaet, O Cho-Cho-San, if you—"

Was this a new doubt? It will never be known.

"Stop! Tha' 's 'nother thing. You got call me O Cho-Cho-San, *an'* Missus Ben-ja-meen Frang-a-leen Pikkerton. Sa-*ay*; you notize how that soun' gran' when my hosban' speaking it that a-ways? Yaes! 'Mos' lig I was a' emperess. Listen! I tell you 'nother thing, which is 'nother secret among you an' me jus': I thing it is more nize to be call that a-way—jus' Missus Ben-ja-meen Frang-a-leen Pikkerton—than Heaven-Descended-Female-

Ruler-Everlasting-Great-Japan, aha! Sa-*ay*; how I loog if I a' emperess? What you thing?"

She imitated the pose and expression of her empress very well.

"If your face liddle longer you loog ezag' lig," said the maid. *again!*

But her mistress was inclined to be more modest.

"Ah, no. *But* I tell you who loog lig a' emperor—jus' ezag'—that Mr. B. F. Pikkerton, when he got that unicorn upon him, with gole all up in front an' down behine!"

And at this gentle treason there was no protest from the patriotic maid.

VII.

How He Didn't Understand Her Whichever!

THE baby continued to sleep. He rather justified the praises of his mother. He was as good as a Japanese baby, and as good-looking as an American one. *Approving. disgusting*

Somebody was without. There was a polite and subdued clattering of clogs in the entrance.

"Gomen nasai" ("I beg your pardon"). *shitsureishimasu.*

It was a familiar, deprecatory voice, accompanied by the clapping of hands. [*she made this up*]

Cho-Cho-San smiled wearily, and called the maid.

"Oh, Suzuki, Goro the nakodo—he is without. Shaka and all the gods defend us now!"

The two exchanged glances of amusement, and the maid proceeded to admit him.

Madame Butterfly received him with the odious lack of ceremony her independent life with Pinkerton had bred. She was imperially indifferent. The go-between pointed out how sad this was to as beautiful a woman as she.

"Is it a trouble to you?" she asked, perking her head aside.

The nakodo only sighed gloomily.

Madame Butterfly laughed.

"Poor, nize liddle old man," said she, with specious pity, in politest English; "do not trouble 'bout me. Do not arrive anymore if it pains you."

"I must; you have no parents now—nor anyone. You are outcast."

"Ah-h-h! *But* will you not permit *me* to suffer the lack?"

"But you will never be married!"

"Again?"

"Well—yes, again, then."

"How tarrible!"

He took this quite seriously, and became more cheerful.

"Yes; a beautiful woman like you must have a husband."

"Yaes. Thangs; I got *one*. Do you perhaps mean more?"

"I mean a Japanese husband."

"Oh—ah? That will have me a month, and then divorce me? And then another, and another, and another?"

She was becoming belligerent.

"How is it better with you now?"

She recovered her good humor.

"At America one is married foraever—*aex*cep' the other die. Aha! What you thing? Your marriages are not so."

She had been speaking indifferently both languages, and now the nakodo, who was not apt at English, begged her to explain this in Japanese. She did so.

"Yamadori has lived long at America, and he says it is not thus. Is it not safe to rely upon his excellent wisdom?"

"No; for I, which am foolish, are wiser than both you an' he. I know. You jus' guess. Aeverybody got stay marry at United States America. No one can git divorce, *aex*cep' he stay in a large court-house, all full judges with long faces, an' bald on their heads, long, long time; mebby two— four—seven year! Now jus' thing 'bout that—*how* that is tiresome! Tha' 's why no one don' git no divorce; they too tire' to wait. Firs', the man he got go an' stan' before those judge, an' tell all he thing 'bout it. Then the woman she got. Then some lawyers quarrel with those judge; an' then the judges git jury, an' as' 'em what they thing 'bout it; an' if they don' know they *all* git put in jail till they git done thinging 'bout it, an' whether they go'n' git divorce or not. Aha!"

"Where did you learn that?" asked the old nakodo, aghast.

"Oh—ah—that Mr. B. F. Pikkerton"—she assumed a grander air— "that Mr. Ben-ja-meen Frang-a-leen Pikkerton—my hosban'—" She smiled engagingly, and held out her pretty hands, as who should say, "Is not *that* sufficient?"

It was so evidently the invention of Pinkerton that it seemed superfluous to make the explanation. The nakodo said curtly that he did not believe it.

Not believe what Mr. B. F. Pinkerton had said!

Cho-Cho-San was exasperated. The engaging smile had been wasted. She flung the blue-eyed baby up before him.

"Well, then, do you believe *that*?"

She laughed almost malignantly. The marriage-broker gulped down this fearful indignity as best he might. He hoped there were not going to be any more such women in Japan as the result of foreign marriages. Still, even this phase of the situation had been discussed with his client.

Why is he?

"But Yamadori, who was bred to the law, tells me that our law prevails in such a matter, the marriage having taken place here."

She gave a gasp, and cried like a savage wounded animal:

"Yamadori—lies!"

The nakodo was silenced. She crushed the baby so fiercely to her breast that he began to cry.

"*Sh!*" she commanded harshly. He looked up for an incredulous instant, then burrowed his head affrightedly into her kimono. She turned upon the nakodo in magnificent scorn.

no

"Oh—*you*—*foo-el!* You thing he naever arrive back. Tha' 's what you thing in secret! He? He *do!*"

She snatched a photograph from an easel at the tokonoma, tore the child from his hiding, and held them up together. Her purpose was quite evident.

The nakodo was thoroughly frightened. She recovered her poise—and her control of the situation.

over done

"*Now* what you thing? Aha, ha, ha! Sa-*ay*— I bed you all moaneys he go'n' come 'mos' one millions mile for see that chile! Tha' 's what I all times praying Shaka an' the augustnesses for—one chile ezag' lig him. *Well*, sa-*ay*! I got him. An' now that Mr. Ben-ja-meen Frang-a-leen Pikkerton he *got* come back—hoarry—even if he don' lig. He cannot stand it. But he do lig."

All her passion was gone now, and her sure gladness returned. She was naive and intimate and confidential again.

"Sa-*ay*! Firs' I pray his large American God,—that huge God-amighty,—but tha' 's no use. He don' know me where I live. Then I pray Shaka an' all the kaimyo of the augustnesses in the god-house. I thing they don' hear me, account they outcasted me when I marry with that Mr. B. F. Pikkerton. *But*"—she smiled at her pretty celestial cajolery—"I pray them so long an' so moach more than they aever been pray with before that they feel good all times, an'—an'"—there was finality in this—"an' 't *is* use. An' mebby I not *all* outcasted! Don' tell him. He—he laugh upon my gods, an' say they jus' wood an' got no works in them. An' he all times call the augustnesses bag nombers! Jus' he don' know till he fine out. Aha, ha, ha!"

"If he returns he will probably take the child away with him—that is his right," chanted the sad-faced nakodo.

But nothing could ruffle Madame Butterfly now. She laughed sibilantly at this owl-like ignorance.

"Oh-h-h! *How* you don' know things! *How* you don' onderstan' me what I mean, whichever! Of course he take that chile away with him—of course! An' *me*—me also; an' Suzuki, aha! An' we go an' live in his castle for aever an' aever!"

The improbability of changing the girl's point of view began to dawn upon the slow intellect of the nakodo.

"At least, Yamadori wishes for a look-at meeting. I have promised him. Will you not grant this?"

Cho-Cho-San shook her head at him knowingly.

"An' if I do not, he not go'n' pay you one present?"

She laughed wildly, and the nakodo by a grin admitted the impeachment.

"Well,"—the spirit of mischief possessed the girl,—"sa-*ay*— I don' keer. Let him come. He lig for see me; I lig for see him. An' if I say I go'n' marry him, he got hoarry an' marry me right away. Aha! What you thing 'bout *those?*"

The nakodo said delightedly that that was precisely what he sought.

"Yaes; *but* suppose they put me in a large jail, an' got loog out between bar—so,"—she illustrated,—"an' don' git nawthin for eat; he go'n' stay all times behind my side, an' comforting me? Hol' my hand? Lemme weep upon him? I dun*no*. Mebby they cut my hade off me. Then he got git his hade cut off, too, an' go the road to Meido together—with—without those hade! Oh, *how* that is tarrible! An' suppose"—she whispered it horridly—"that Mr. B. F. Pikkerton—aha, ha, ha!—*arrive?*"

The nakodo was not sure how much of this was meant seriously. They were extremely unusual humors to him. But she had consented to the meeting, and he promptly took her at her word.

"When, then, will it please you to have me bring Yamadori?"

"When you lig—nize liddle ole friend."

The nakodo fixed that day a week.

As he was going, Cho-Cho-San laughingly asked:

"Sa-*ay*! How often he been marry?"

"But twice," the nakodo replied virtuously.

"An' both times divorce?"

He admitted that this was the case.

"An' both times jus' on visit from United States America—jus' *liddle* visit?—so long?" She spread her hands.

Under her laughing gaze it seemed best to admit it.

"Oh! *he*—he jus' marry 'nother for *fun*—whenever he thing 'bout it. Then he forgit it when he don' thing 'bout it, and marry another. Say so!"

He heard her laugh again as he left the courtyard; but he had confidence in the ability of Yamadori to accomplish his purpose if he could be brought into contact with her. He was one of the modern pensioned princes of Japan, a desirable matrimonial article, and preternaturally fascinating.

No one would want Cho Cho San now, no matter how beautiful. Her honor is lost. Yamenori would not be interested in reality.

VIII.
The Bright Red Spot in Cho's Cheeks

THE look-at meeting came about as planned. There was a distinct air of state about Madame Butterfly's house on that day. The baby, and all the frivolities that attended him, were in banishment. The apartment had been enlarged by the rearrangement of the shoji. At the head of it, statuesque in her most brilliant attire, sat Cho-Cho-San. Japanese women are accomplished actresses; and looking in upon Cho-Cho-San just at the moment of Yamadori's arrival, one would not have known her. She was as unsmiling, as emotionless, as the Dai-Butsu. *large beast (?)*

The grave ceremonies attending the advent of a candidate for matrimony went forward with almost no recognition from Cho-Cho-San until they had come to the point where they might seat themselves before her, to inspect and be inspected. Then she struck her fan against her palm, and Suzuki appeared, and set the tobacco-bon between them.

Yamadori suggested somewhat the ready-made clothier[12]—inevitable evidence of his transformation; otherwise he was the average modern Japanese, with high-gibbeted trousers, high collar, high hat, and eyeglass. He might not converse directly with Cho-Cho-San, especially concerning the business at hand; but he was not prohibited from conferring with the nakodo about it in her presence. The rule of decorum for such an occasion simply decreed that she should be blind and deaf concerning what went on. The convenience of the arrangement is obvious. The nakodo, the representative of both parties, was happily permitted, on the part of the one, to regard what was happening as if it had not happened, and, on the part of the other, as if it had.

"She is quite as beautiful as you said," remarked Yamadori, after a careful inspection with his glass.

---

[12] Ready-made clothing was available only beginning in the mid-nineteenth century; the wealthy continued to have their clothes custom-tailored. The implication here is that Yamadori is dressed in the current Western style, but that his clothing fits poorly and is cheaply made.

The nakodo nodded virtuously, and filled his pipe. His client lighted a cigarette.

Cho-Cho-San did not even smile.

"And her father, you say, was on the emperor's side in the Satsuma rebellion?"[13]

The marriage-broker satisfied his client to the last particular of her father's bloody sacrificial end at Jokoji.

"And you have told her faithfully of *me*?" He paused on the last word to note its effect upon Cho-Cho-San. There was none, and he hastened to add cumulatively, "And my august family?" He paused again. But again there was no sign from the lady of the house. She was staring out over his head. "And have offered her my miserable presents?"[14]

To each of these the broker answered, lugubriously, yes.

"Then why, in the name of the gods, does she wait?"

The nakodo explained with a sigh that she had declined his presents.

"I will send her others. They shall be a thousand times more valuable. Since I have seen her I know that the first must have been an affront."

She kept her eyes up, but Yamadori unquestionably smiled in the direction of Cho-Cho-San—as if she were a woman of joy!

The light of battle came into the stony eyes of the girl. She clapped her hands almost viciously. The little maid appeared.

"Tea!" she said.

The maid brought the tea; and with that splendid light of danger still in her eyes, Cho-Cho-San served it. With the air of a princess she put on in an instant all the charms of a mousmee. She gave back smile for smile now, and jest for jest. She begged Yamadori, with the most charming upward inflections, to put away his cigarette and take her shippo pipe, and he did it. *That* was Japanese, she said, his cigarettes were not. Was it not so?—with a resistless movement toward him. She let him touch her hands in the passage of the cups. She enveloped him with the perfume of her garments. She possessed him wholly in one dizzy instant.

"I will give her a castle to live in," said Yamadori, breathlessly.

---

[13] In the Satsuma rebellion of 1877, a group of samurai from the southwestern region of Kyushu, led by Saigo Takamori, rose up against the Meiji regime, which had replaced the feudal estates of the shogunate with a European-style national government in 1871. The government troops, trained in Western warfare, easily defeated the samurai, and after the final battle on Tahara-zaka hill, Saigo committed ritual suicide at Shiroyama. Because of his heroism, his treason was posthumously pardoned by the Meiji emperor.

[14] These gifts, which Yamadori presents with false modesty as "miserable presents," were to be given by Yamadori to Cho-Cho-San in exchange for her hand in marriage.

The nakodo sighed. Cho-Cho-San refilled his pipe with an incomparable grace.

"Ah!" she permitted her lips to breathe—very softly.

"She shall have a thousand servants."

There was no audible response from the nakodo, but his eyes gleamed avidly.

Cho-Cho-San returned the pipe, smiling dazzlingly. It seemed almost yes with her.[15]

"Everything her heart can wish!" cried Yamadori, recklessly.

The nakodo turned beseechingly toward the girl. She lifted her eyebrows. He did not understand. As she passed him she laughed.

"Is it enough?"

Still he did not understand.

"Have we earned the present?" she whispered.

"I will give a solemn writing," added Yamadori, fervidly.

"She still fancies herself, perhaps, married to the American," sighed the nakodo.

Yamadori laughed disagreeably.

"If Your Excellency would condescend to explain—"

"Oh, she is not serious. A sailor has a sweetheart in every port, you know."

Cho-Cho-San whispered something to the nakodo. She still smiled.

"But she is perhaps his *wife*," answered he, obediently.

"Yes," said Yamadori, as if they were the same.

Cho-Cho-San whispered again.

"But the child—there is a most accomplished child?" said the nakodo.

"Yes," said the traveled Japanese, with the same smile and the same intonation.

There was a distinct silence. Cho-Cho-San smiled more vividly. But her nostrils moved rapidly in and out. The nakodo grew anxious. Yamadori cast his eyes toward the ceiling, and continued:

"A sailor does not know the difference. In no other country are children esteemed as they are here. In America it is different. People sometimes deny them. They are left in a basket at some other person's door. But the person does not receive them. They are then cared for by the municipality as waifs. It is shameful to be such a child. There are great houses and many officers in each city for the care of these. They are an odious class by themselves, and can never rise above their first condition."

---

[15] That is, it seemed she was assenting to the marriage proposal.

The nakodo glanced askance at his client. He had not the slightest objection to a man who would lie a little to win his cause, but to lie too much was to lose it.   *It was no lie.*

"I myself knew a man whose child became a cripple. He sent him to the mayor of the city, saying that as the cars of the city had injured him, the city must bring him up. He was sent to the poorhouse, and afterward to the stone-quarries. It was a most piteous sight."

Cho-Cho-San bent again to the ear of the old man. There was a tremor in her voice now.

"Had he eyes of purple?" asked the nakodo.

"He was beautiful of face; but surely eyes of purple are not desirable?" Yamadori brought his own down from the ceiling and leveled them at Cho-Cho-San. She still smiled, but there was a bright-red spot in each cheek now. "But he was misshapen, and he was never known to laugh. I saw many such. I saw a child whose father had deserted it, and the mother—"

Madame Butterfly clapped her hands again. The maid appeared promptly; she had expected the summons.

"Suzuki—good Suzuki, the excellent gentlemen—the august"—she swept a royal gesture toward them—"who have done us the honor to call, they wish to go hurriedly. Their shoes—will you not hasten them?"

With a final brilliant smile she turned her back upon them and left the room.

"Your story of the rejected child did it," reproached the nakodo, on the way back.

"I had not got to the worst," said his client, ruefully. "I meant to cite an example exactly to suit her own case."

"Lucky she turned us out when she did, then."

"What do you mean, sir?" demanded the suitor, in sudden wrath.

"Oh," said the broker, in polite haste, "I was beginning to feel—ill."

The irony of this escaped the client. Still, Goro would have had a less opinion of Yamadori if, having lied once, he had not lied again in defense of the first.   *Is this sarcasm?*

Though Yamadori came no more, he had brought the serpent to Madame Butterfly's Eden.

IX.
"'Bout Birds"

ONE day she took her courage, and the maid's too, for that matter, in both hands, and called upon the American consul. She saw the vice-consul. There was a west wind, and it was warm at Nagasaki. He was dozing. When he woke, Madame Butterfly was bowing before him. At a little distance was the maid with the blond baby strapped to her back. He was unable to account for them immediately. — *would not be blonde*

"Goon night," said Cho-Cho-San, smiling amiably.

The consul glanced apprehensively about. "Night! Not night, is it?"

They both discovered the error at the same instant.

"Ah! no, no, no! Tha' 's *mis*-take. Me—I'm liddle raddle'. Aexcuse us. Tha' 's not nize, mak' *mis*-take. We got call you good morning, I egspeg, or how do? What you thing?"

"Whichever you like," he answered, without a smile.

Then Cho-Cho-San waited for something further from the consul. Nothing came. She began to suspect that it was her business to proceed instead of his.

"I—I thing mebby you don' know me?" she questioned, to give him a chance.

"Oh, yes, I do," declared the consul. In fact, everybody knew her, for one reason and another—her baby, her disowning, her beauty, her "American" marriage. "You are O Cho-Cho-San, the daughter—" he forgot her father's name, though he had often heard it. "You used to dance, did you not?"

"Aha! See! Tha' 's what I thing. You don' know me whichaever. I nobody's daughter; jus' Missus Benja—no! Missus Frang-a-leen Ben-ja-meen—no, no, *no*! Missus Ben-ja-meen Frang-a-leen Pikkerton. Aeverybody else outcast me. Aha, ha, ha! I liddle more raddle'."

"Oh!" The consul was genuinely surprised, and for the first time looked with interest at the child. Cho-Cho-San, to aid him, took Trouble from the maid. Finally he politely asked her what he could do for her.

"I got as' you a thing."

She returned the baby to the maid.

"Proceed," said the consul.

"You know 'bout birds in your country?"

"Yes, something."

"Ah! tha' 's what I thing. You know *aevery*thing. Tha' 's why your country sen' you here—account you ver' wise."

"You do me too much honor," laughed the consul.

"You—*don'*—know?"

She was distinctly alarmed.

"Everything? No; only a few things."

"*But* you know ''bout birds—*robins*—jus' liddle robins?"

Her inflections denounced it a crime not to know. He was not proof against this, or against these.

"Oh, yes," he said; "of course."

"Aha! Of course. Tha' 's what I all times thinging. Tha' 's *mis*-take by you?"

They could laugh together now.

"Ah! Tell me, then, if you please, when do those robin nest again? *Me?* I thing it is later than in Japan, is it not? Account—jus' account the robin nesting again jus' *now* in Japan."

The consul said yes because the girl so evidently desired it—not because he knew.

"Aha! Tha' 's what I thing. Later—moach later than in Japan, is it not?"

Again her fervid emphasis obliged him to say yes, somewhat against his conscience.

"An'—sa-*ay*! When somebody gitting marry with 'nother body at your America, don' he got stay marry?"

"Usually—yes; decidedly yes; even sometimes when he doesn't wish to." *No.*

"An' don' madder where they live?"

"Not at all."

"Ah-h-h! *How* that is nize! Sa-*ay*; you know all 'bout that. What you thing?"

"Well, I know more about that than about ornithology. You see, I've been married, but I've never been a—a robin."

The joke passed quite unnoticed. She put her great question:

"An' no one can't git divorce from 'nother *aex*cep' in a large court-house full judge?"

"Yes," laughed the consul; "that is true."

"An' that take a ver' long time?"

"Yes; nearly always. The law's delay—"

"An' sometimes they git inside a jail?"

She was so avid that she risked the very great discourtesy of an inter-ruption—and that, too, without a word of apology. Suzuki was, for an in-stant, ashamed for her.

"Occasionally that happens, too, I believe."

Every doubt had been resolved in her favor.

"An' if they got a nize bebby yaet—don' they—ah, don' *aever*body lig that?"

"I did, very much. Mine is a fine boy."

"Sa-*ay*! He loog lig you—purple eye, bald hairs, pink cheek?"

"I'm afraid he does."

"'Fraid?"

"Glad, then."

"Oh! 'Fraid mean glad? Yaes. Tha' 's way Mr. B. F. Pikkerton talking— *don'* mean what he say an' don' say what he mean—ezag'." *Stupid sense of humor diff. from INDIRECT Japanese way.*

The consul laughed, but he could not quite understand the drift of her questioning.

"If people have a nize bebby alig that, they don' give him away, not to nob'y—nob'y—they don' *lig*? What you thing?" *this is so backwards & confused.*

"I should think not!" For a moment he looked savage as a young father can.

Cho-Cho-San's face glowed. She stood consciously aside, that the con-sul might better see the baby on Suzuki's back. He understood, and smiled in the good-fellowship of new parenthood. He made some play with the child, and called him a fine fellow.

"Ah! You naever seen no soach bebby, I egspeg?"

In the largess of his fellowship he declared that he had not. He had only recently been engaged in putting the same question to his friends. She had hoped, indeed, that he would go on from that and say more, the subject so abundantly merited it; but she now remembered that, in her haste to satisfy her doubts, she had neglected all those innumerable little inquiries which go to make up the graceful game of Japanese courtesy. Though she might neglect them with Pinkerton, she must not with a stranger who was obliging her.

X.

Gentle Lying

"Ah! How is that health? Also, I am sawry I woke you up, excellent, an' that I interrup' your languages. That is not a happy for the most exalted health—to be wake up an' interrup'. Therefore, I pray your honorable pardon. An'—how *is* that health?"

The consul said that he was quite well.

"Ah, *how* that is nize! An' you always sleeping well, most honorable?"

He nodded.

"Yaes—I hear you sleep. Oh! Tha' 's not joke! No, no, no!"

He had laughed, but she would never do that.

"But I do—snore, I believe—sometimes."

He was not proud of even this, of course.

"*Oh*! jus' lig gentle breezes."

He said that he could not do better than adopt this charming euphemism.

"Also, how ole you gitting ver' soon?"

"Thirty."

A Japanese always adds a few years.[16] She therefore thought him younger, and her veneration abated accordingly. But he was in fact older.

"Tha' 's also nize—ver' nize. I wish I so ole. That Mr. B. F. Pikkerton he lig me more if I older, I thing." She sighed.

"I don't know about that. The American point of view differs." But he would not meddle. "How old are you, pray?"

This was only the proper return for her courtesy. Besides, the consul was enjoying the usually dull game of decorum to-day. The girl was piquant in a most dazzling fashion.

"Me? I 'bout—'bout—" (what he had said made her doubt a little the Japanese idea) "'bout 'mos' twenty-seven when the chrysanthemum blooms again."

She was seventeen.

---

[16] Long implies that a Japanese would add years to his or her age when asked, to elicit the respect accorded to older people in their society.

"Yaes, 'bout 'mos' — twenty-seven" — with a barely perceptible rising inflection.

He acquiesced in the fiction, but smiled at the way she hung her head and blushed; this was not the Japanese way of telling one's age (or any other gentle lie).

"You got a grandmother?" she proceeded.

"Two," alleged the consul.

"Tha' 's ver' splen-did. An' is she well in her healths also?"

"Which one?"

She passed the joke, if she saw it. No Japanese will make his parent the subject of one.

"The ole one — always the ole one firs'."

The consul felt queerly chidden.

"She was well at last accounts."

"Tha' 's nize. An' the young one?"

"The same. And now, about yours?"

"Alas! I have not that same happiness lig you. I got not ancestors whichever. They all angery account that Mr. B. F. Pikkerton, so they outcast me out the family. He don' lig that they live with him, account they bag nombers. He an' me go'n' be only bag nomber, he say. He big boss bag nomber, me jus' liddle boss bag nomber. *Me?* I don' got ancestors before me nor behine me now. Hence they don' show me the way to Meido when I die. Well, me? I don' keer whichaever. I got hosban' an' bebby tha' 's mos' bes' nize in Japan, mebby in the whole world. An' I kin go at Nirvana by 'nother road, aha! if I moast."

The kindly consul, better than she, understood both the effect of this separation of her from her "ancestors," and the temperament of Pinkerton. He undertook, notwithstanding his resolution not to meddle, a tentative remonstrance. She listened politely, but he made no impression.

"You must not break with your relatives. If Pinkerton should not, should — well, die, you know, you would indeed be an outcast. If your own people would have nothing to do with you, nobody else would. It must, of course, be known to you that your — marriage with Pinkerton has put you in unfortunate relations with everybody; the Japanese because you have offended them, the foreigners because he has. What would you do in such a case?"

"Me? I could — dance, mebby, or — or die?" No.

But she laughed as she said it. Then she acknowledged his rebuking glance.

"*Ae*xcuse me, tha' 's not—nize? Well, it is not so easy to die as it was—before he came." She sighed happily.

The consul was curious.

"Why?" he asked.

"Why?—He make my life more sweet."

"But that is no reason for quarreling with your family."

"*But* they don' wan' *me*, because my hosban' don' wan' *them*! Henceforth I got go 'way from my hosban' if I wan' them; an' if I wan' him more bedder, I got go 'way from them. No madder whichaever, I got go 'way from *some* one. Well, I wan' those hosban' more bedder than any. Sa-*ay*! Tha' 's a foanny! They make me marry with him when *I* don' wish him; now I am marry with him, *they* don' wish him. Jus' after my father he kill his self sticking with short sword, tha' 's how we gitting so poor—oh, ver' poor! Me? I go an' dance liddle, so we don' starve. Also, I thing if somebody wish me I git married for while, account that grandmother got have food an' clothings. *Well*, those ver' grandmother she as' the ole nakodo 'bout it; she lig me git marry with someone. He say mans jus' as' him other day kin he git him nize wife, an' he don' know none nizer."

She paused to let the consul make sure of this fact, which he did, and then acknowledged the appreciation she had provoked with a charming smile.

"Whichaever, he say he thing I don' lig him, account he America-jin, he also remarking with me that he a barbarian an' a beas'. *Well*, me?—I say I don' wan' him. I 'fraid beas'. *But* aeveryone else they say yaes—yaes, ah, yaes—he got *moaney*, an' for jus' liddle while I got endure him. So I say, 'Bring me that beas'.' An' lo! one day the ole nakodo he bringing him for look-at meeting. *Well!*—"

She paused to laugh, and so infectious was it that the consul adventurously joined her.

"At firs' I thing him a *god*, he so tall an' beautiful, and got on such a blue clothes all full golden things. An' he don' sit 'way, 'way off, an' jus'—*talk*!"

She laughed abandonedly.

"He make my life so ver' joyous, I thing I *nae*ver been that happy."

She had an excess of demureness.

"Oh, jus' at firs' I frighten'; account he sit so *close* with me—an' hol' my han'—an' as' if it made satin. Aha, ha, ha! Satin! Loog!"

She gave them both to him. They were deliciously pretty; but the consul was embarrassed by his possession of them. She began slowly to withdraw them, and then he let them go with regret.

"I beg your august pardon. I jus' thinging in the inside me, an' speaking with the outside. Tha' 's not nize. You don' keer nothin—'bout—that—those?"

"What?"

He thought she meant the hands—and perhaps she did.

"Jus' those—liddle—story."

"Yes, I do," declared the consul, with some relief; "it is a charming story." And it was, for Cho-Cho-San's eyes and hands took part in its telling as well as her lips.

"You mean—you lig hear more?"

"Yes." No.

She reflected an instant.

"I thing there is no more. Jus'—yaes, jus' after while I naever git frighten' no more—no madder how close, nor how he hol' my hand."

"But then you—I beg pardon—you were married? I think you said so?"

"Oh, yaes," she replied, as if that had made little difference in their situation; "I marry with him."

"I think his ship was then ordered to—"

She nodded.

"Alas! he got go an' serve his country. But he go'n' come back, an' keep on being marry with me. What you thing?"

The consul contrived to evade the interrogation.

"Is that why you asked about the robins?"

"Yaes; he go'n' come when the robins nest again. *He?* He don' naever egspeg we got this nize bebby, account I don' tell him. I don' kin tell him. I don' know where he is. But—*me?* I don' tell if I know, account he rush right over here, an' desert his country, an' henceforth git in a large trouble—mebby with that President United States America, an' that large Goddess Liberty Independence! What you thing?"

XI.

"The Mos' Bes' Nize Man"

IT was quite superfluous to point out such of her ideas as had birth in the fertile brain of Pinkerton. Certainly he had enjoyed his married life with her, but it was for another reason than hers. The consul could observe, he thought, how exquisitely amusing it had been. It was, too, exactly in Pinkerton's line to take this dainty, vivid, eager, formless material, and mold it to his most wantonly whimsical wish. It was perhaps fortunate for her that his country had had need of him so soon after his marriage.

However, the consul informed her that her fears of trouble for Pinkerton from the sources mentioned were entirely groundless. But this, to his surprise, was not pleasing intelligence. She liked to believe (as he had let her believe) that Pinkerton occupied a large space in the affairs of his country; that he was under the special patronage of the President, and the Goddess of Liberty was, perhaps, her own corollary. But it fitted his character as she had conceived it. To her he was a god, perhaps. But let it be understood that a Japanese god is neither austere nor immaculate.

"Well, whichaever," she said, in some disappointment, "tha' 's a so'prise on him when he come. He all times joking with me; I make one joke upon him. Tha' 's good joke. What you thing?"

The consul shook his head. The matter began to have a sinister look. But the girl's faith was sublime.

"Ah-h-h! *You?*" Her inflection was one of pity for his ignorance. "Tha' 's account you don' know him, you shaking your nize head. He joking all times. Sometime I dunno *if* he joking, *aex*cep' he stop, look solemn, an' laugh. *Then* he make the house raddle! Oh, mebby you thing I don' joke too, also? Well, tha' 's *mis*-take. I make joke jus' lig him—jus' bad. One time I make joke with him 'bout run 'way to that grandmother, account I don' keer for him no more. *Well*—what you thing? He say, "Ello! Less see how you kin run fas'.' Aha, ha, ha! Tha' 's liddle joke upon me. Now I go'n' have the larges' joke upon him. Sa-*ay*—you got tell him, if you please, augustness, that I couldn't wait, it was so long—long—long! I got tire'. So—I am marry with a great an' wise prince name' Yamadori Okyo, an' live in a huge castle with one thousan' servants, an'—an' all my hearts kin wish! Aha, ha, ha! Also, that I go'n' away to his castle with his purple-eye' bebby, to naever return no more—naever. You go'n' tell him that?"

"I would prefer not to have a hand in any further—that is, any deception," the consul objected gravely.

The girl was amazed and reproachful.

"Ah-h-h! Don' you lig joke? I thing aevery American do. Tha' 's not nize for me. I got be sawry I telling you all those. Alas! *How* that would be nize for you! You see him git angery so quick." She smote her hands together. "An' then he say those remark 'bout debbil an' hell, an' rush up the hill this-away."

She again lifted her kimono, and acted it recklessly across the apartment. Mercury poisoning?

"But, my dear madame—"

She came at him with a voice and movement that were resistlessly caressing. He perceived how useless it would be to protest further. He acknowledged her protean fascination.

"Ah-h-h! *Please*, augustness, to tell him? It will be that *nize* for me! Ah, you go'n' do it?—*Yaes?* Say so!"

The consul had capitulated to her voice and eyes. This was evident to her.

"Ah—thangs, most excellent. You the mos' bes' nize man in the worl'—"

She paused guiltily; even this purely Japanese euphemism might be conjugal treason.

"Except?" laughed the consul.

"*Aex*cep'," confessed the girl, with drooping head.

A smile began to grow upon her lips; when she raised her face it was a splendid laugh.

"*How* we have fun seeing him rush up that hill at the house"—she was frankly dissembling—"so!" She illustrated again—back and forth across the apartment. "After that—ah—after that—*well*—I make aeverything correc'."

She was radiantly certain that she could.

The consul remembered the saying of the professor of rhetoric that no comedy could succeed without its element of tragedy. Well, Pinkerton *might* have meant to return to her. Any other man probably would. He would not have been quite certain of himself. Only, that stuff about the robins sounded like one of his infernal jokes. He probably supposed that she knew what he meant—farewell; but she had not so construed it.

Unless Pinkerton had changed, he had probably not thought of her again—except as the prompt wife of another man. He never explained anything. It was his theory that circumstances always did this for one; it was therefore a saving of energy to permit circumstances to do it. There was a saying in the navy that if anyone could forget a played game or a spent bottle more quickly than Pinkerton, he had not yet been born. Providing her with a house and money meant nothing. He would probably have given her all he had, whether it were a dollar or a thousand. But, on the other hand, if she had been one of the sudden and insane fancies which occasionally visited him, the case was altogether different, and altogether like Pinkerton; for in the person of a fascinating woman the emotion might survive the absence in question. For himself, he was quite sure—had he been Pinkerton, of course—that it would have survived something greater. And finally his own views prevailed with him as if they were Pinkerton's, and he believed that he would be delighted to return and resume his charming life with her on Higashi Hill.

He thereupon told her that Lieutenant Pinkerton's ship was under orders to stop at Nagasaki, the government rendezvous for the navy, about the first of September, to observe and report the probabilities of war with China; and he was instantly glad that he had told her.

The girl's superb joy was expressed in a long, in-drawn sigh, and then silence.

But something had to be said—or done.

"I—I lig as' you 'nother thing—" again dissembling, as if the talk were still at the trivialities where it began.

"Certainly," said the consul, with a smile. "But won't you have a chair?"

He had noticed that she was trembling. She sat up unsteadily on the edge of it. And then she forgot what she meant to ask!

"Sa-*ay*!" She was still at sea. But suddenly a thought flashed in her eyes. "All bebbies at your America got those purple eye?"[17]

"A—yes, very many of them," said the consul, with a little surprise at her direction.

"An'—an' also bald of their head?"

"All of them, I believe, at first."

He smiled, and the girl smiled back at him engagingly.

"Sa-*ay*, augustness, he go'n' come for see those bebby? What you thing?" Her words were like caresses.

---

[17] Long characterized mixed-race children as having purple eyes in other texts, including a story titled "Purple Eyes," which was published in the same volume as *Madame Butterfly*.

But the rapture growing surely in the girl's face now was not reflected in that of the consul. Concern for her outweighed her fascinations for the moment.

"I—I hope so—"

She cut off his doubting incontinently.

"Sa-*ay*! Mebby you also don' thing he go'n' take us live in his large castle at United States America?" she challenged reproachfully.

"Did he tell you that he would—that he had one?"

"No; he don' tell me—*naw*thing. He laugh, when I as' him, lig the house go'n' fall down. *But*—what you thing?"

The consul answered her quite briefly. He knew that he hurt her, but his impotent anger was at Pinkerton; he had not thought him capable of that.

"If I were to advise, I should ask you to consider seriously Yamadori's proposal, if he has really offered himself. It is a great and unusual opportunity for you—for any girl—in—in Japan."

"You—thing—those—? *You*?"

She looked at him for an amazed and reproachful instant; then gathered her kimono in her hand, and pushed her feet into her clogs.

"Go before, Suzuki," she said gently to the maid; to the consul, sorrowfully, "Goon night."

At the door she turned with a ceremonial sweep of her draperies, looked, and came hurrying back. All the joy had returned to her face at the sincere regret—almost pain—she saw upon his. She impulsively grasped his hands—both of them.

"Once more—different—goon night, augustness." And her voice was very soft. "Aha, ha, ha! *Me*? I jus' a foo-el—*yaes*. *You*?—you the mos' bes' nize man in all the whole worl'—"

She paused—smiling up at him. He understood that she wished to repeat their pretty play upon the phrase.

"Except?"

She nodded and laughed.

"*Aex*cep'—Ha, ha, ha!"

She hurried after the maid, laughing back at him confessingly as she went.

And, after all, the consul was glad it had ended thus. For joy is better than sorrow—always and everywhere.

When they again reached the pretty house on the hill, Cho-Cho-San looked ruefully back over the steep road they had come.

"Oh, *how* that was tiresome, Suzuki! But *he*—when he comes, it will

be jus'—one—two—three great strides! *How* he will rush up that hill it
cost us so much sweat to climb! Lig storm with lightening and thunder!
Flash! flash! flash! Boum! boum! boum! An' here he is—all for jus' liddle
me! Then *how* he will stamp about—not removing his boots—spoiling the
mats—smashing the fusuma—shaking the house lig earthquake animal!
'Where is she? Hah! Mans tole me she gone an' marry with a fool Yamadori! Gone me my purple-eye' bebby away.' Then I jump roun' his
neck before he gitting *too* angery, an' hole his han', an' say, close with his
ears: 'How do, Mr. B. F. Pikkerton?' Aha, ha, ha! What you thing,
Suzuki?"

And Suzuki said, in English, too:

"Tha' 's mos' bes' nize thing *I a*ever see!"

XII.

Like a Picture of Bunchosai

From that time until the seventeenth of September not a ship entered the harbor but under the scrutiny of the glass that Lieutenant Pinkerton had left at the little house on Higashi Hill to read his signals aboard. And there were very many of them, for the war was imminent. Faith had begun to strain a little with unfaith, after the first. It was very long; but on the seventeenth his ship came into the bay. So like a great bird did she come that the glass did not find her until her white-and-gold mass veered to make an anchorage. Then, all at once, the gilt name on her bow was before Cho-Cho-San's eyes. It was tragically sudden. With a hurtling cry, she fell to the floor. The little maid, with Eastern intuition, understood; but she said nothing, and did—what was best. Both she and her mistress—and all the world, for that matter—knew the comfort of this speechless, sympathetic service. And presently she was better, and could talk.

"I—I di'n' know I *so*—glad," softly laughed Cho-Cho-San.

But the maid had known what to expect.

"You go'n' res' liddle now, please, Oku-San![18] You go'n' sleep liddle—please, jus' liddle—res'—sleep?"

She drew her mistress's eyelids down, and lightly held them. Cho-Cho-San shook her off, and sprang up, revivified.

"Res'! Sleep! Not till he come!"

"Res'—peace—sleep—*beauty*," chanted the maid, persuasively. But her mistress would not.

"Now, hasten lig you got eagle's wings an' a thousan' feet! It will not be one hour—not one half—till he will be here. My pink kimono—widest obi—kanzashi for my hair—an' poppies. I will be more beautiful than I have aever been. Flowers—alas! there are no cherry-blossoms. *How* that is sad! Seem lig we cannot be gay without them. In the month of the cherry-blossoms we were marry! But chrysanthemums—all of them! An' lanterns if it be black night—'mos' one thousan'! Aha, ha, ha! His house

---

[18] *Okusan* is Japanese for "wife."

shall be gayer than it has aever been. There shall naever again be such good occasion."

"Res' is beauty," urged the maid, holding up the mirror to her.

"Ah, Suzuki! I *am* beautiful—as beautiful as when he went away?"

The maid was silent—the Japanese silence which is *not* assent.

Cho-Cho-San savagely snatched the metallic mirror out of her hand.

"I *am*!" she cried. "Say so!"

She brandished the heavy mirror over the girl's head.

"I as' you to res'—peace—sleep. Tha' 's way git beautiful once more."

"Oh-h-h! 'Once more'!" The mirror crashed to the floor, and she burst into tears.

"Jus'—you been too trouble'. Now you go'n' res' liddle," urged the comforting maid.

"Oh, all the gods! I cannot!—I cannot till he come. I shall die before."

She sorrowfully recovered the mirror.

"No—no; pitiful Kwannon, I am no longer beautiful! Waiting an' doubting make one soon sad an' old. An' how long we have wait!—how long! Oh, Shaka! But now I am happy—happier than I have aever been. Therefore shall I be more beautiful than I have aever been again. For happiness also is beauty. Ah, Suzuki, be kine with me!" She got on her knees to the maid, and laid her head at her feet. An ecstatic thought came to her. "Suzuki, *you* shall make me beautiful to-day, an' to-morrow the gods shall. Now we have not even time to pray them—not time to res'. Will you not? Can you not? Ah-h-h! You *moast*!"

She pulled the girl down to her, and whispered the last words in her ear—with her arms about her.

And the girl did. Let us not inquire how. She had never yet withstood that tone and that caress. There was a certain magic in her deft fingers, and her mistress had it all. No daintier creature need one ever wish to see than this bride awaiting anew the coming of her husband.

And when it was all done, they each took a final delighted look into the mirror. It was too small to show the whole figure, but they moved it up and down and round about until every portion had been seen. They both pronounced it very good.

"Stan' jus' that way," begged the maid, going the length of the apartment to observe. "Jus' lig those new porcelains of Kinkozan!"[19] she declared.

---

[19] Kinkozan was a Japanese maker of fine pottery during the Edo and Meiji periods (nineteenth-early twentieth centuries).

"Jus' lig those ole picture of Bunchosai!"[20] retorted Cho-Cho-San—meaning anything but that.

But—in the way of women the world over—a few more touches were necessary—and it was finished.

"Now the flowers for his room! Take them all—oh, aevery one! We shall not need them again. Go—go—*go*! Aha, ha, ha! An' Trouble—make a picture of him! He will be Trouble no longer after to-day. He go'n' git new name—mebby Joy!—Joy!"

Her commands were obeyed. Within the appointed hour the house was decked as for a festival, and not a flower remained upon its stem. The baby had indeed become a picture; and so had Cho-Cho-San and the maid and the house.

Then they hid behind the shoji, recklessly making peep-holes with their dampened fingers, as they had planned. There was one very low down for the baby, so that he could sit on the mats,—which he did not choose to do,—and one each for the others.

Cho-Cho-San sang as she fixed herself at her peep-hole—so as not to disarrange her finery:

> "Rog-a-by, bebby, off in Japan,
> You jus' a picture off of a fan."

The maid tossed the baby like a ball into her lap.

"Aha, ha, ha!" laughed Madame Butterfly once more.

Everything was at last quite as they had planned it.

"Now let him come," she said, in a charming defiance—"let him come—quickly—an'—then—"

The hour passed. Then two—four. Night fell. They ceased to chatter. Later came perfect silence; then that other silence of the dead of the night. The pulses of terror quickened. Suzuki noiselessly lighted the lanterns. Later, at a shivering gesture from her mistress, she lighted the andon in their room; then the hibachi. She had grown very cold. All night they watched. He had the careless habit of the night. But he did not come.

And all the next day they watched, and many after, quite silent now, always. The baby wondered at this, and would look inquiringly from one to the other. It was very strange to him, this new silence. The house had been

---

[20] Probably a reference to Bunsei Gaishi, a Japanese painter from the Muromachi period (fifteenth century).

full always of their laughter and chatter—the patter of their feet—the sighing of the shoji. They did nothing now but watch—and eat a little, sleep a little—less and less of these. Finally Cho-Cho-San could no longer hold the glass. She lay on the mats with the baby, while the faithful handmaid watched. Every day the faded flowers were replaced by purchased ones— cheaper and cheaper ones. Their last money went for this and the candles which renewed the lights of the lanterns each night. These were not a thousand—were not a dozen—now.

She did not think of going to him. In destroying her Japanese conventions this was the one thing that had been left. In "Onna Yushoku Mibea Bunko" ("The Young Ladies' Old Book of Decorum") she had read that the only woman who seeks a male is a yujo, a courtesan.

In a week a passenger-steamer came into the bay. They took no interest in her. But the next day, quite by accident, they saw him for the first time. He was on the deck of the strange ship. A blonde woman was on his arm. They watched quite sleeplessly all that night. A few more lanterns were lighted.

On the following morning the warship had disappeared from the harbor.

Cho-Cho-San was frightened. The sinking at her heart she now knew to be black doubt. Her little, unused, frivolous mind had not forecast such a catastrophe. There might have been a reason, she had conceived, for his detention aboard his ship. He was never very certain. She had not been sure that he was with her until the day before; the position of the vessel had been unfavorable for observation.

XIII.

The Good Consul's Compassionate Lying

DEMORALIZATION set in. Even the comfort of the maid was dulled. They decided that Cho-Cho-San should go to see the good consul, while the maid and the baby remained at home to welcome him if, perhaps, he had not gone with the warship. They had already created this hope.

The maid helped her down the steepest part of the hill. Nevertheless, when she arrived at the consulate she was quite breathless. The consul was alone. There were no frivolities now. Each knew that the other understood.

"Me? I got—liddle heart-illness, I thing," the girl panted in excuse of her lack of ceremony and the consul's pitying stare. She looked very ill; but her smile was still tragically bright.

The consul placed her a chair. She declined it. There was a moment of conscious silence. Then he went hesitatingly to his desk, and got an envelope containing money—a large sum. He silently handed her this.

She looked at him in appealing inquiry, but she did not take the money.

"It is only—only in remembrance of the—the past. He wishes you to be always happy—as—he says he is. He confidently hopes for your good wishes and congratulations."

There was moisture in the consul's eyes, only questioning in hers. He suddenly saw that she did not understand. He decided that she never should. He did not speak again, nor did she for a space. Then:

"Happy—happy?" she murmured dizzily. "*But*—how kin *I* be happy if he do not come? How kin *he* be—happy—if—he do not come?"

The consul was silent. He still held the money toward her. She tried to smile a little, to make him think she was indifferent concerning his answer to the question she was about to ask.

"Ah—oh—*ah*! You tole him 'bout—'bout that joke—that liddle joke we make on him?"

The consul pretended ignorance. She explained:

"That 'bout me go'n' marry with Yamadori, an' take his bebby 'way?"

He had to answer now:

"Oh, that was—too—too foolish to talk about seriously."

Pinkerton had been glad to hear it.

"But—you—*tole* him?"

She hoped now he had not.

"Well—"

He looked out of the window. He would not strike, but she would be struck.

"But—you—you *tole* him?" She had raised her voice piteously.

"Yes," answered the consul, dully, wondering what he could say next.

She gasped, and wiped her dry lips.

"Yaes; tha' 's—right. Tha' 's—what I—as' you do. An'—an' what he—say?" she questioned huskily.

The consul was willing to lie as deeply as the occasion might demand. The woe in the girl's face afflicted him. He saw in her attire the pitiful preparations to welcome the husband he now knew to be a craven [soul], and in her face what it had cost to wait for him. But in specie the lie was difficult.[21]

"Well," he began uncertainly, "we—it all happened about as you had supposed. He got very angry, and would have rushed right up the hill, as you thought, only—only—" What next? The wish to lie had grown upon him wondrously as he went on. But invention flagged. The dispatches on his desk caught his eye. "Only—he was not permitted a moment's leave while in the harbor. He had all these dispatches to prepare for—for his government—the war, you know. All in cipher."

He showed them to her. A brilliant thought came into his head.

"See! They are all in his handwriting."

He had not written a line of them.

"His ship was ordered away suddenly to China; but he'll be back here one of these fine days, and then—"

The rest was for her. At any rate, he could lie no more.

"All—all the gods in heaven bless—you," she said, sinking with the reaction.

She reeled, and he put her into the chair. Her head fell limply back, and her pallid face looked up at him with the weary eyes closed. But there was rest and peace on it, and it was still very beautiful.

Someone was approaching in haste, and he drew a screen before her.

---

[21] That is, he found it difficult to lie in the reality of the moment.

XIV.

The Blonde Woman

A woman entered.

"Mr. Sharpless—the American consul?" she asked, while crossing the threshold.

The consul bowed.

"Can you reach my husband at Kobe—by telegraph?"

"I think so. Who is your husband?"

He took up a writing-pad as he spoke.

"Lieutenant Pinkerton of the—"

"One moment, for God's sake!"

It was too late. The eyes of the little woman in the chair were fixed on his. They even tried to smile a little, wearily, at the poor result of his compassionate lying. She shook her head for silence.

"I beg your pardon; I'm—I am—ready—" said the consul, roughly. He made no other explanation. "Proceed."

"I should like you to send this telegram: 'Just saw the baby and his nurse. Can't we have him at once? He is lovely. Shall see the mother about it tomorrow. Was not at home when I was there to-day. Expect to join you Wednesday week per *Kioto Maru*.[22] May I bring him along? ADELAIDE.' "

As she advanced and saw Cho-Cho-San, she stopped in open admiration.

"How very charming—how *lovely*—you are, dear! Will you kiss me, you pretty—*plaything*!" Isn't this bizarre by any standard?

Cho-Cho-San stared at her with round eyes—as children do when afraid. Then her nostrils quivered and her lids slowly closed.

"No," she said, very softly.

"Ah, well," laughed the other, "I don't blame you. They say you don't do that sort of thing—to women, at any rate. I quite forgive our men for falling in love with you. Thanks for permitting me to interrupt you. And, Mr. Sharpless, will you get that off at once? Good day!"

---

[22] The name of the ship that will take her to him incorporates the name of the city that is now spelled "Kyoto."

She went with the hurry in which she had come. It was the blonde woman they had seen on the deck of the passenger-steamer.

They were quite silent after she was gone—the consul still at his desk, his head bowed impotently in his hands.

Cho-Cho-San rose presently, and staggered toward him. She tried desperately to smile, but her lips were tightly drawn against her teeth. Searching unsteadily in her sleeve, she drew out a few small coins, and held them out to him. He curiously took them on his palm.

"They are his, all that is left of his beautiful moaney. I shall need no more. Give them to him. I lig if you also say I sawry—no, no, *no!* glad— glad—*glad!*" She humbly sighed. "*Me?* I—I wish him that happiness same lig he wish for himself—an'—an'—me. *Me?* I shall be happy— mebby. Tell him I—shall be—happy."

Her head drooped for a moment. When she raised it she was quite emotionless, if one might judge from her face.

"Thang him—that Mr. B. F. Pikkerton—also for all that kineness he have been unto me. Permit me to thang *you*, augustness, for that same. You—you"—she could smile a little now at the pretty recollection—then the tears came slowly into her eyes— "you—the mos' bes' nize man—in all the—whole—worl'."

She closed her eyes a moment, and stood quite still.

The consul said below his breath:

" ——Pinkerton, and all such as he!"[23]

"Goon night," said Cho-Cho-San, and at the door looking back, "Sayonara," and another tired smile.

She staggered a little as she went out.

"Alas, you also have seen her!" wailed the intuitive little maid, as she let her mistress in.

"An' she is more beautiful than the Sun-Goddess," answered Cho-Cho-San.

The maid knelt to take off her shoes.

"She—she thing me—jus' a—plaything."

She generously tried to smile at the maid, who was weeping. She touched her hair caressingly as she knelt.

"Don' weep for me, liddle maiden—account I disappoint—a liddle— disappoint—don' weep for me. That liddle while ago you as' me to res—

---

[23] The long dash signifies a curse, probably "damn."

peace—sleep," she said after a while, wearily. "Well, go 'way, an' I will—res'. Now I *wish* to res'—sleep. Long—long sleep. An' I pray you, loog, when you see me again, whether I be not again beautiful—again as a bride."

The maid did not go. Once more she understood her mistress.

"*But*— I thing *you* loave me?"

The girl sobbed.

"Therefore go—that I suffer no more. Go, that res'—peace—sleep. Long—beautiful sleep! Go, I beg."

She gently took her hands and led her out.

"Farewell, liddle maiden," she said softly, closing the shoji. "Don' weep."

XV.
When the Robins Nest Again

SHE sat quite still, and waited till night fell. Then she lighted the andon, and drew her toilet-glass toward her. She had a sword in her lap as she sat down. It was the one thing of her father's which her relatives had permitted her to keep. It would have been very beautiful to a Japanese, to whom the sword is a soul. A golden dragon writhed about the superb scabbard. He had eyes of rubies, and held in his mouth a sphere of crystal which meant many mystical things to a Japanese. The guard was a coiled serpent of exquisite workmanship. The blade was tempered into vague shapes of beasts at the edge. It was signed, "Ikesada."[24] To her father it had been Honor. On the blade was this inscription:

> To die with Honor
> When one can no longer live with Honor.

It was in obscure ideographs; but it was also written on her father's kaimyo at the shrine, and she knew it well.

"To die with Honor—" She drew the blade affectionately across her palm. Then she made herself pretty with vermilion and powder and perfumes; and she prayed, humbly endeavoring at the last to make her peace. She had not forgotten the missionary's religion; but on the dark road from death to Meido it seemed best now to trust herself to the compassionate augustnesses, who had always been true.

Then she placed the point of the weapon at that nearly nerveless spot in the neck known to every Japanese, and began to press it slowly inward. She could not help a little gasp at the first incision. But presently she could feel the blood finding its way down her neck. It divided on her shoulder, the larger stream going down her bosom. In a moment she could see it making its way daintily between her breasts. It began to congeal there. She pressed on the sword, and a fresh stream swiftly overran the other—redder, she thought. And then suddenly she could no longer see it. She drew

the honor ?

"painlessness" completely false !

---

[24] The name of the sword-maker.

the mirror closer. Her hand was heavy, and the mirror seemed far away. She knew that she must hasten. But even as she locked her fingers on the serpent of the guard, something within her cried out piteously. They had taught her how to die, but he had taught her how to live—nay, to make life sweet. Yet that was the reason she must die. Strange reason! She now first knew that it was sad to die. He had come, and substituted himself for everything; he had gone, and left her nothing—nothing but this.

The maid softly put the baby into the room. She pinched him, and he began to cry.

"Oh, pitiful Kwannon! Nothing?"

The sword fell dully to the floor. The stream between her breasts darkened and stopped. Her head drooped slowly forward. Her arms penitently outstretched themselves toward the shrine. She wept.

"Oh, pitiful Kwannon!" she prayed.

The baby crept cooing into her lap. The little maid came in and bound up the wound.

When Mrs. Pinkerton called next day at the little house on Higashi Hill it was quite empty.

A Japanese Nightingale

•

Onoto Watanna

"The Storm Dance." From A Japanese Nightingale *by Onoto Watanna (New York: Harper and Bros., 1901). Illustrated by Genjiro Yeto.*

CONTENTS

I.

The Storm Dance

THE last rays of sunset were tingeing the land, lingering in splendor above the bay. The waters had caught the golden glow, and, miser-like, seemingly made effort to keep it with them; but, inexorably, the lowering sun drew away its gilding light, leaving the waters a dark green. The shadows began to darken, faint stars peeped out of the heavens, and slowly, unwillingly, the day's last ray followed the sunken sun to rest; and with its vanishment a pale moon stole overhead and threw a seraphic light over all things.

Out in the bay that the sun had left was a tiny island, and on this a Japanese businessman, who must also have been an artist, had built a teahouse and laid out a garden. Such an island! In the sorcerous moonlight, one might easily believe it the witch-work of an Oriental Merlin. Running in every direction were narrow jinrikisha roads, which crossed bewildering little creeks, spanned by entrancing bridges. These were round and high, and curved in the center, and clinging vines and creeping, nameless flowers crawled up the sides and twined about the tiny steps which ascended to the bridges. After crossing a bridge shaped thus, a straight bridge is forever an outrage to the eye and sense. And all along the beach of this island was pure white sand, which looked weirdly whiter where the moonbeams loitered and played hide-and-seek under the tree-shadows.

The seekers of pleasure who made their way out to the little island on this night moored their boats here in the shadows beneath the trees, and drove in fairy vehicles, pulled by picturesque runners, clear around the island, under the pine-trees, over miniature brooks, into the mysterious dark of a forest. Suddenly they were in a blaze of swinging, dazzling lights, laughter and music, chatter, the clattering of dishes, the twang of the samisen, the ron-ton-ton of the biwa. They had reached the garden and the teahouse.

Some pleasure-loving Japanese were giving a banquet in honor of the full moon, and the moon, just over their heads, clothed in glorious raiment, and sitting on a sky-throne of luminous silver, was attending the banquet in person, surrounded by myriad twinkling stars, who played at being her courtiers. Each of the guests had his own little mat, table, and waitress. They sat in a semicircle, and drank the sake hot, in tiny cups that went thirty or more to the pint; or the Kyoto[1] beer that had been ordered for the foreigners who were the chief guests this evening. This is the toast the Japanese made to the moon: "May she with us drink a cup of immortality!" and then each wished the one nearest him ten thousand years of joy.

Now the moon-path widened on the bay, and the moon itself expanded and grew more luminous as though in proud sympathy and understanding of the thousand banquets held in her honor this night. All the music and noise and clatter and revel had gradually ceased, and for a time an eloquent silence was everywhere. Huge glowing fire-flies, flitting back and forth like tiny twinkling stars, seemed to be the only things stirring.

Someone snuffed the candles in the lanterns, and threw a large mat in the center of the garden, and dusted it extravagantly with rice flour. Then a shaft of light, that might have been the combination of a thousand moonbeams, was flashed on the mat from an opening in the upper part of the house, and out of the shadows sprang onto the mat a wild, vivid little figure, clad in scintillating robes that reflected every ray of light thrown on them; and, with her coming, the air was filled with the weird, wholly fascinating music of the koto and samisen.

She pirouetted around on the tips of the toes of one little foot, clapped her hands, and curtsied to the four corners of the earth. Her dance was one of the body rather than of the feet, as back and forth she swerved. There was a patter, patter, patter. Her garments seemed endowed with life, and took on a sorrowing appearance; the lights changed to accompany her; the music sobbed and quivered. It had begun to rain! *She* was raining! It seemed almost as if the pitter-patter of her feet were the falling of tiny raindrops; the sadness of her garments had increased, and now they seemed to be weeping, at first gradually, then faster and still faster, until finally she was a storm—a dark, blowing, lightning storm. From above the light shot down in quick, sharp flashes, the drums crashed madly, the koto wept on, and the samisen shrieked vindictively.

Suddenly the storm quieted down and ceased. A blue light flung itself against the now lightly swaying figure; then the seven colors of the spectrum flashed on her at once. She spread her garments wide; they fluttered about her in a large half-circle, and, underneath the rainbow of the gown,

[1] Kyoto is a city in southwest Japan with over a thousand temples.

a girl's face, of exquisite beauty, smiled and drooped. Then the extinction of light—and she was gone.

A common cry of admiration and wonder broke out from Japanese and foreigners alike. They called for her, clapped, stamped, whistled, cheered. One man's voice rose above the clatter of noises that had broken loose all over the gardens. He was demanding excitedly of the proprietor to tell him who she was.

The proprietor, smirking and bowing and cringing, nevertheless would not tell.

The American theatrical manager lost his head a moment. He could make that girl's fortune in America! He understood it was possible to purchase a geisha for a certain term of years. He stood ready on the spot to do this. He was ready to offer a good price for her. Who was she, and where did she live?

Meanwhile the nerve-scraping dzin, dzin, dzin of a samisen was disturbing the air with teasing persistence. There is something provoking and still alluring in the music of the samisen. It startles the chills in the blood like the maddening scraping of a piece of metal against stone, and still there is an indescribable fascination and beauty about it. Now as it scratched and squealed intermittently and gradually twittered down to a zoom, zoom, zoom, a voice rose softly, and gently, insinuatingly, as it entered into the music of the samisen. Only one long note had broken loose, which neither trembled nor wavered. When it had ended none could say, only that it had passed into other notes as strangely beautiful, and a girl was singing.

Again the light flashed down and showed her standing on the same mat on which she had danced, her hands clasped, her face raised. She was ethereal, divinely so. Her kimono was all white, save where the shaft of moonbeams touched the silk to silvery brilliance. And her voice! All the notes were minors, piercing, sweet, melancholy—terribly beautiful. She was singing music unheard in any land save the Orient, and now for the first time, perhaps, appreciated by the foreigners, because of that voice— a voice meant for just such a medley of melody. And when she had ceased, the last note had not died out, did not fall, but remained raised, unfinished, giving to the Occidental ears a sense of incompleteness. Her audience leaned forward, peering into the darkness, waiting for the end.

The American theatrical manager stalked towards the light, which lingered a moment, and died out, as if by magic, as he reached it. But the girl was gone.

"By Jove! She's great!" he cried out, enthusiastically. Then he turned on the proprietor.

"Where is she? Where can I find her?"

The man shook his head.

"Oh, come, now," the American demanded, impatiently, "I'll pay you."

"I don' know. She is gone."

"But do you know where she lives?"

The proprietor again answered in the negative.

"Now, wouldn't that make one of this country's squatty little gods groan?" the exasperated manager demanded of a younger man who had followed him forward.

"She'd be a great card in vaudeville," the young man contented himself with saying.

"There's a fortune in her! I'm going to find her if she's on this island. Come on with me, will you?"

Nothing loath, Jack Bigelow fared forth behind the theatrical man, whom he had never seen before that afternoon, and whom he never expected to see again. They hurried down one of the narrow, shadowy roads that almost made a labyrinth of the island. But fortune was with them. A turn in the road, which showed the waters of the bay not fifty yards ahead, revealed just in front of them two figures—two women— both small, but one a trifle taller than her companion.

"Hi there! You!" shouted the manager, who, though among a people whose civilization was older than his own, considered them but heathen, and gave them the scant courtesy deserved by all so benighted in matters theatrical. The two figures suddenly stopped.

"Are you the girl who sang?"

"Yes," came the answer in a clear voice from the taller figure.

The manager was not slow in coming to the point.

"Would you like to be rich?"

Again the positive monosyllable, uttered with much eagerness.

"Good!" The manager's face could not be seen, but his satisfaction was revealed in his voice. "Just come with me to America, and your fortune's made!"

She stood silent, her head down, so that the manager prompted her impatiently: "Well?"

"I stay ad Japan," she said.

"Stay at Japan!" The manager barely controlled himself. "Why, you can never get rich in this land. Now look-a-here—I'll call and see you to-morrow. Where do you live?"

"I don' want you call. I stay ad Japan."

This time the manager, seeing a possible fortune escaping him, and having in mind the courtesy due the heathen, delivered himself of a large Christian oath. "If you stay here, you're a fool. You'll never—"

The young man named Bigelow, who had watched the attempted bargaining in silence, broke in with some indignation. "Oh, let her go! She's got a right to do as she pleases, you know. Don't try to bully her into going to America if she'd rather stay here."

"Well, I suppose I can't use force to make her take a good thing," said the manager, ungraciously. He drew out his card-case and handed the girl his card. "Perhaps you'll change your mind after you think about this a bit. If you do, my name and Tokyo address are on that card; just come round and see me. I'm going down to Bombay to look out for some Indian jugglers. I'll be gone about five months, and will be back in Tokyo before I start out on another trip to China, Korea, and the Philippines, and then off for home."

The girl took the card and listened in silence; when he finished, she curtsied, slipped a hand into that of her companion, and hurried down the narrow road.

After the two Americans had made their way back to the tea-garden, the older one at once sought out the proprietor.

"You know something about that girl. Come, tell us," he said, imperiously.

The proprietor was profusely courteous, but hesitated to speak of the one who had danced and sung. Finally he unbent grudgingly. He told the theatrical man and his companion that he knew next to nothing about her. She had come to him a stranger and had offered her services. She refused to enter into the usual contract demanded of most geishas, and in view of her talents he could not afford to lose her. She was attracting large crowds to his gardens by her strange dances. Still he disliked and mistrusted her. She came only when it suited her whim, and on *fêtes*[2] and occasions of this kind he had no means of knowing where she was. It was only by accident she had happened in this evening. Once he had attempted to follow her, but she had discovered him, and made him promise never to do such a thing again, threatening to stay away altogether if he did so.

"Beautiful, excellencies! Phow! You cannot see properly in the deceitful light of this honorable moon. A cheap girl of Tokyo, with the blue-glass eyes of the barbarian, the yellow skin of the lower Japanese, the hair of mixed color, black and red, the form of a Japanese courtesan, and the heart and nature of those honorably unreliable creatures, alien at this country, alien at your honorable country, augustly despicable—a half-caste!"

---

[2] French for "celebrations."

II.

In Which Woman Proposes and Man Disposes

Jack Bigelow was beset by the nakodas (professional match-makers). He was known to be one of the richest foreigners in the city, and the nakodas gave him no rest. Though he found them interesting, with the little comedies and tragedies to relate of the matches they had made and unmade, he had remained impregnable to their arts. He naturally shrank from such a union, and in this position he was strengthened by a promise he had made before leaving America to a college chum, his most intimate friend, a young English-Japanese student, named Taro Burton, that during his stay in Japan he would not append his name to the long list of foreigners who for a short, happy, and convenient season cheerfully take unto themselves Japanese wives, and with the same cheerfulness desert them.

Taro Burton was almost a monomaniac on this subject, and denounced both the foreigners who took to themselves and deserted Japanese wives, and the native Japanese, who made such a practice possible. He himself was a half-caste, being the product of a marriage between an Englishman and a Japanese woman. In this case, however, the husband had proved faithful to his wife and children up to death; but then he married a daughter of the nobility, a descendant of the proud Jokichi family, and the ceremony had been performed by an English missionary. Despite the happiness of this marriage, Taro held that the Eurasian[3] was born to a sorrowful lot, and was bitterly opposed to the union of the women of his country with men of other lands, particularly as he was Westernized enough to appreciate how lightly such marriages were held by the foreigners. It was true, of course, that after the desertion the wife was divorced, according to the law, but that, in Taro's mind, only made the matter more detestable.

---

[3] The term Eurasian entered English usage in the mid-nineteenth century, and referred primarily to children of English and Indian descent (a by-product of British colonial rule in India). Both Eaton and her sister Edith (writing under the pseudonym Sui Sin Far) used the term to refer to themselves and their mixed-race characters of Chinese and Japanese descent. See Winnifred's short story "A Half-Caste" and Edith's autobiographical essay "Leaves from the Mental Portfolio of an Eurasian." (CIT).

For five years, up to their graduation four months before this, the young American and the young half-Japanese had been associated as closely together as it is possible for two young men to be, and a strong and deep affection existed between them.

It had been originally decided that the friends would make this trip together, which in Taro Burton's case was to be his return to the home he had left, and, with Jack Bigelow, was to be the beginning of a year's travel preliminary to entering the business of his father, who was a rich shipbuilder. But for some reason, which he never clearly set forth to his friend, Taro had backed out at almost the last minute; yet he had urged Jack to undertake the trip alone, and, under promise to follow shortly, finally had prevailed. So Jack Bigelow had made the long voyage to Japan, and had taken a pretty house of his own a short distance from Tokyo.

It was unfortunate that Taro could not have accompanied his friend, for while the latter was not a weak character, he was easy-going, good-natured, and easily manipulated through his feelings.

The young Japanese, had he done nothing else, at least would have kept the nakodas and their offerings of matrimonial happiness on the other side of the American's doors. As it was, one of them in particular was so picturesque in appearance, quaint in speech, and persistent in his calls, that the young man had encouraged his visits, until a certain jocular intimacy put their relations with each other on a pleasant and familiar footing.

It was this nakoda (Ido was his name, so he told Jack) who brought an applicant for a husband to his house one day, and besought him at least to hold a look-at meeting with her.

"She is beautiful like unto the Sun-goddess," he declared, with the extravagance of his class.

"The last was like the moon," said the young man, laughing. "Have you any stars to trot out?"

"Stars!" echoed the other, for a moment puzzled, and then, beaming with delighted enlightenment, "Ah, yes—her eyes, her feet, hair, hands, twinkling like unto them same stars! She prays for just a look-at meeting with your excellency."

"Well, for the fun of the thing, then," said the other, laughing. "I'm sure I don't mind having a look-at meeting with a pretty girl. Show her into the zashishi (guest-room) and I'll be along in a moment. But, look here," he continued, "you'd better understand that I'm only going through this ceremony for the fun of the thing, mind you. I don't intend to marry anyone—at all events, not a girl of that class."

"Nod for a leetle while whicheven?" persuaded the nakoda.

"Nod for a leetle while whicheven," echoed the young man, but the agent had disappeared.

When Jack, curious to know what she was like, she who was seeking him for a husband, entered the zashishi, he found the blinds high up and the sunshine pouring into the room. His eyes fell upon her at once, for the shoji at the back of the room was parted, and she stood in the opening, her head drooping bewitchingly. He could not see her face. She was quite small, though not so small as the average Japanese woman, and the two little hands, clasped before her, were the whitest, most irresistible, and perfect hands he had ever seen. He had heard of the beauty of the hands of the Japanese women, and was not surprised to find even a girl of this class—she was a geisha, of course, he told himself—with such exquisite, delicate hands. He knew she was holding them so that they could be seen to advantage, and her little affected pose amused and pleased him.

After he had looked at her a moment, she subsided to the mats and made her prostration.[4] She was dressed very gaily in a red crêpe kimono, tied about with purple obi. Her hair was dressed after the fashion of the geisha, with a flower ornament at the top and long, pointed daggers at either side; but as she bowed her head to the mat, some pins in her hair escaped and slipped, and then a tawny, rebellious mass of hair, which was never meant to be worn smoothly, had fallen all about her, tumbled into her eyes and over her ears, and literally covered her little crouching form. She shivered in shame at the mishap, and then knelt very still at his feet.

Bigelow was speechless. Never before in his life had he seen such hair. It was black, though not densely so, for all over it, even where it had been darkened with oil, there was a rich red tinge, and it was luxuriously thick and long and wavy.

"Good heavens!" he said, after the little figure had remained absolutely motionless for a full minute, "she'll hurt or cramp herself in that position."

The girl did not rise at the sound of his voice, but crept nearer to him, her hair still enshrouding her. It made him feel creepy, and annoyed and pleased and amused him altogether.

"Don't do that," he said. "Please stand up. Do!"

The nakoda told him to lift her to her feet, and the young man did so, entangling his hands in her hair. When she stood up, he saw her face,

---

[4] A Japanese greeting of deep respect.

which was oval and rosy, the lips very red. She still drooped her eyes, so that her face was incomplete.

"What's your name?" he asked her, gently. "And what do you want with me?"

Now she raised her head and he saw her eyes. They startled him. They were large, though narrow, and intensely, vividly blue. Before, with her hair neatly smoothed and dressed, he had noticed nothing extraordinary about her; now, with that rich red-black hair enshrouding her, and the long, blue eyes looking at him mistily, she was an eerie little creature that made him marvel. A Japanese girl, with such hair and eyes! And yet the more he looked at her, the more he saw that her clothes became her; that she was Japanese despite the hair and eyes. He did not try to explain the anomaly to himself, but he could not doubt her nationality. There was no other country she could belong to.

"You are Japanese?" he finally asked, to make sure.

She nodded.

"I thought so, and yet—"

She smiled, and her eyes closed a trifle as she did so. She was all Japanese in a moment, and prettier than ever.

"You see—your eyes and hair—" he began again. She nodded and dimpled, and he knew she understood.

"What is it you want with me?" he asked, desiring rather to hear her speak than to learn her object, for this he knew.

She was solemn now. She flushed, and her eyes went down. To explain to him why she had come to him in this wise was a painful task. He could guess that, but she forced the words past her lips.

"To be your wife, my lord," she said in English, and the queer quality of her voice thrilled him strangely.

This was the answer he knew was coming; nevertheless it stirred him in a way he had not expected. To have this wonderfully pretty girl before him, beseeching him to marry her—he who had as yet never dreamed of marriage for himself—was disturbing to his balance of mind. Nay, more—it was revolting. He shrank back involuntarily, wondering why she had come to him, and this wonder he put into words.

"But why do you want to marry me?" he asked.

The expression of her face was enigmatical now. She had ceased to blush and smile, and had become quite white. Suddenly she commenced to laugh—trilling, elfish laughter that rang out through the room, startling the echoes of the house.

"Why?" he repeated, fascinated.

She shrugged her shoulders. "I mus' make money," she said.

Of course this was her reason; he knew that before she spoke; but hearing her say so gave him pain. She was such a dainty little body.

"Oh, you need not sell yourself for that," he said earnestly. "Why, I'll give you some—all you want. You're awfully young, aren't you? Just a little girl. *I* can't marry you. It wouldn't be fair to you."

Again she shrugged her shoulders, and spoke in Japanese to the nakoda.

"She says someone else will, then," he interpreted.

"All right," said the young man, almost bitterly.

She pretended to go towards the door, and then came back towards Bigelow.

"I seen you before," she announced, ingenuously.

"Where?" He was curiously interested. He fancied that her face was familiar.

"Ad tea-house."

"What tea-house?"

"On liddle bit island. You 'member? I dance like this-a-way." She performed a few steps.

"What! You that girl?" He knew her in an instant now. "How could you remember me?"

"You following me after dance with 'nudder American gent, and before thad someone point ad you—ole wooman thad always accompanying me."

"How did *she* know me?"

"She din' know you to speag ad, bud—she saying you mos' reech barbarian ad all Japan."

"Oh, I see," he said, coldly.

"She tell me I bedder git marry with you."

"Indeed! Why?"

She hung her head a moment. "Because she know I luffing with you," she said.

"You loving with *me*!" He laughed outright. Her ingenuousness was entrancing.

"Yes," she said, and he, with masculine conceit, half believed her.

"But wouldn't you rather stay at the tea-house than get married?" he asked.

"Not nuff money that businesses," she returned.

"Do you do everything for money?"

"How I goin' to live?" This question, answering a question, brought her back to the purpose of her visit. She held her little hands out to him.

"Ah, excellency, *pray* marry with me," she begged.

He took her hands quickly in his own. They were soft and so small. He could enclose them with one of his. They were delightful. He knew they were daintily perfumed, like everything else about her. He did not let them go.

"You ought not to marry, you know," he said to her, almost boyishly. "How old are you, anyhow?"

She ignored his question.

"I will be true, good wife to you forever," she said, and then swiftly corrected herself, as though frightened by her own words. "No, no, I make ridigulous mistage—not forever—jus' for liddle bit while—as you desire, augustness!"

"But I don't desire," he laughed nervously. "I don't want to get married. I won't be over but a few months at most in Japan."

"Oh, jus' for liddle bit while marry with me," she breathed entreatingly. "Pl-ease!"

It hurt him strangely to have her plead so. She looked delicate and refined and gentle. He put her hands quickly from him. She held them out and put them back again into his. Her eyes clouded, and he thought she was going to cry.

He was seized with a desire to keep her from weeping, if he could, this little creature, who seemed made for anything but tears.

He spoke from this impulse, without giving so much as a second's thought to the seriousness of his words.

"Don't cry. I'll marry you, of course, if you want me to."

He felt the hands in his own tremble.

"Thangs, excellency," she said, in a voice that was barely above a whisper, but it was a voice which had in it no note of joy.

There was pleasure, however, in the eyes of the nakoda. He had done a good piece of business, a most excellent piece of business, for the American gentleman was reputed to be able to buy hundreds and hundreds of rice-fields if he so cared to do. The nakoda came forward with a benignant smile to arrange the terms.

"She will cost only three hundred yen per down and fifteen yen each end per week. Soach a cheap price for a wife!"[5]

---

[5] The equivalent to approximately $600 in today's currency. The fifteen yen per week ostensibly refers to the "allowance" provided to the new wife. Eaton makes clear throughout these negotiations how little the "marriage for jus' liddle while" differed from prostitution.

It was the grinning face of this matrimonial middleman that brought Bigelow back to his senses. He had said he would marry this little creature, whose limp hands he was holding. He dropped them as though they were the hands of one dead, and drew back.

"I won't do it!" he almost shouted. "Never!" Then he thought what must be the feelings of the little girl whose yoke of marriage he was refusing, and softened. "I wasn't thinking when I said I would. I don't want to marry a Japanese girl. I don't want to marry any girl. I wouldn't be doing right, and it wouldn't be fair to you." He paused, and then added, lamely, "I think I'd like you awfully, though, if I only knew you."

"But—" spoke up the nakoda, anxiously, who found his dream of a large fee fading into thin air.

Jack turned upon him quickly and gave him a sharp look, whereat he retired hurriedly.

A look of relief had come over the girl's face when Jack had cried out that he would not marry her, and at this he wondered much. This relief in her face, however, was succeeded almost instantly by disappointment. But she spoke no further word. She gave him a single hurried glance from beneath fluttering eyelashes, curtsied until her head was almost on a level with his knees, and left him.

III.

An Appointment

JACK Bigelow regarded the attempt of the nakoda and little Miss— (he had not even thought to ask her name) as an incident closed by the retirement of the one aspiring to wifehood from his sight. But in passing from his house she had not passed from his mind. This she occupied in spite of him, though it must be said that Jack made no effort to eject her.

He had been approached by many nakodas, who had the disposal of some most excellent wives, so they had told him, but never before had he consented to see one of their offerings; so the sensation of being asked in marriage by a girl whom he had only seen once before, and that under circumstances which prevented his seeing her clearly, was altogether new. That he, John Hampden Bigelow, A.B.—he was very proud of that A.B., it had not cost him any particular labor—should be so sought out was not at all displeasing to his vanity, a quality that he prided himself on not possessing; this, notwithstanding the fact that he knew he had been approached because he had money.

He chuckled at the event several times during the day. He would keep this incident in mind, with all its detail, and make use of it now and then after he had returned home, when he was called upon to talk of his experiences in other lands. Of course, he would exaggerate a bit here and tone down a bit there and would make the girl much prettier. No, the girl was pretty enough. This part of the incident could not be improved upon.

Jack mused about the morning's episode during the entire day, and twice exploded into such laughter at the idea of his being asked for a husband that his little man[6] hurried in to see if the gray-eyed barbarian was taking leave of his senses. In the evening he grew restless, and, having nothing else to do—so he told himself—he went out to the tea-garden on the little island which he had visited a few nights before. For an hour he waited for something—for something that did not appear. Finally, when the proprietor chanced to pass him, he asked in the manner of one casually interested:

"The girl who danced and sang the other night—is she here?"

---

[6] That is, his manservant.

She was not, for which the proprietor humbly asked pardon. She had not visited his poor place since the night the American had seen her.

For some reason Jack suddenly lost interest in the house and gardens, and returned to his home. But the next night—again because he had nothing else to do—found him once more a guest at the tea-garden. This time he did not leave at the end of an hour; possibly because a weird dance was performed and a weird song, sung by a girl with vivid blue eyes. He could not see their color from where he sat, but he knew they were blue.

After that he fell into the habit of visiting the gardens every night— these were dull times in Tokyo—never anything else to do. Most of the evenings so spent were intensely wearisome, but some few of them were not. It may only have been a series of coincidences, but it so happened that on the enjoyable evenings there was a weird dance and a weird song, and on the others there were not the graceful swayings of a little body, nor the wonderful music of a wonderful voice.

One evening, immediately after the song had been ended, he found himself striding down the same road that he had taken with the excited theatrical manager, and this without consciously having decided upon such a course. But he came down to the beach without seeing man or woman, and, though he would not acknowledge to himself that he was seeking anyone, he carried away with him a keen sense of disappointment.

For two weeks the dullness of Tokyo remained unabated, so that the evenings offered nothing else to do save to go to the tea-gardens. At the end of that time, Jack, becoming honest with himself, admitted that there was nothing else, because there was nothing else he wanted to do, and while in this frank mood he let it become known to himself that there was nothing else in all the land of the rising sun that held so much of interest to him as did the girl who had offered herself to him for a wife—nothing, indeed, in all the other lands of the earth. Why this was, he did not know, not being one given to searching his own soul or the souls of others.

While he reclined at his ease one afternoon in the little room in which he lounged and smoked, he began to place her, in his imagination, here and there in the house, to try the effect. He set her in one of his largest chairs, notwithstanding she would have been much more comfortable on the floor,[7] in this same room, and she added wonderfully to the appearance of things. He stood her pensively by the tokonama; he nodded his

---

[7] Here Eaton alludes to the Japanese custom of sitting on cushions on floors rather than in Western-style chairs.

head—very good! He placed her out beneath a cherry tree in his garden; again he nodded approvingly. And a breakfast with her sitting opposite him! That would be like unto the breakfasts eaten by the angels in heaven—if angels partake of other than spiritual nourishment. Yes, she would be wonderfully effective in his little house, would harmonize with it greatly.

But what an odd figure she would make in an American dress! He thought of her in a golfing costume, and smiled at his fancy. Nevertheless, even in the gowns worn by the women of his own country, she would be quaint and charming, he felt sure. She would be awkward, of course, but would be graceful even in her awkwardness. And she would transgress every polite convention, and would make herself all the more delightful in so doing. He compared her to the wives of some of the men he knew, to many of the girls he had met since girls had begun to have interest for him, and his admiration for her grew apace. He would be proud of her, he knew, for she was pretty and would attract attention; men like their wives to draw eyes towards them. She was unlike the wife of any of his countrymen he was likely to meet, and this also was much.

What would his parents think? They'd be angry at first, of course, but they'd give in; they loved him, and couldn't resist her; no one could resist her. Anyhow, this prospective trouble was so far ahead that there was no use in wasting thought upon it now.

Why the deuce hadn't he learned her name? It was very monotonous, this being compelled to think of her only as "she" and "her."

But why had she come to him asking him to marry her? He shook his head at that; he didn't quite like it. But—oh well, you know, these Japs have no end of queer customs. This incident just illustrated one of them. She was clearly a superior kind of a girl. Not an ordinary geisha as he had thought when his eyes first fell on her. He had seen enough of the geishas at the tea-houses to know that she was of a different kind; to his Occidental eyes these last were most pleasing creatures, but—

Just then his man straggled through the room and brought an end to his musing. Marry her? He sat up straight. What had he been thinking about? The idea was absurd. It was absurd for him to think about marrying anyone. He got to his feet, called back his man, and ordered a jinrikisha to be brought to him. He rode off to Tokyo to forget all about it.

But it would not be forgotten. After he had left the jinrikisha he caught sight of her on the opposite side of the street, turning a corner. He hurried after her, but when he reached the corner she was nowhere to be seen. He looked into all the shops on either side of the street for a distance of a hundred yards, but saw no one who bore the least resemblance to her. Then he tramped about the immediate vicinity, his sense of loss deepening with each minute, until he noticed that the shop-keepers were eyeing him with suspicion. He gave up the search and started back to his jinrikisha.

As he was swinging along disconsolately, his eyes lighted upon another person whom he knew—Ido, the nakoda—and him Jack did not let escape. He pounced down upon him, and clapped a hand upon his shoulder.

"Hallo there!" he called out.

Ido started back as if he had been set upon by an enemy. He was unused to such emphatic greetings. But when he saw who his assailant was he slipped a smile upon his face, smirked and bowed, and hoped that the august American's days were filled with joy.

"They'll do," Jack answered. "And how are things with you? Business good? Making many matches?" Ido had introduced four persons to incomparable happiness—which was to say, he had brought about two marriages. Had his lordship come into like happiness?

No, his lordship had not.

"You making gradest mistage you' whole lifetime," Ido assured him. "You nod yit seen Japanese woman that please you for wife? No? I know 'nudder girl you' excellency nod seen yit. Mos' beautiful in Japan. You like see her?"

"No, I've seen enough. By the way, Ido, what's become of the girl you brought around to my place? Married yet?" Jack put on a look of indifferent interest.

"No, excellency."

For one disinterested, Jack found much relief in this answer.

"But I thing she going to be," Ido went on, calmly. "Two, three—no, two odder gents—what you say?—consider—yes, consider her."

These words drove relief from the disinterested Jack's heart, and instantly set up in its place a raging jealousy. But he compelled himself to remark, quite easily, "You don't say!"

Ido confirmed his statement with a nod that was almost a bow.

"A very pretty girl," Jack commented, loftily.

Ido's reply was confined to a mere "Yes." There was no use going into ecstasies when no bargain was in sight.

"I think I'll go around to see her, and congratulate her," Jack went on, "Where does she live?"

"I regretfully cannot tell."

"Ah, well, let it go then. But, say, I really would like to see her again before she's married. Rather took a fancy to her, you know. Couldn't you bring her to call on me tomorrow morning?"

"I going to be very busy tomorrow." Seeing no chance of earning a marriage-fee, he saw no reason for taking the trip.

"I'll pay you for your trouble—needn't worry about that."

Perhaps Ido could arrange to come; yes, now that he thought again, he knew he could come.

So it was settled that he and the girl should visit Jack at ten o'clock the next day.

IV.

In Which Man Proposes

THE announcement of his man that Ido and his charge had arrived contained no news for Jack, for he had been watching the road from Tokyo since nine o'clock, and had seen them while they were yet afar off. Nevertheless, he did not enter the zashishi until his man came to him with word that guests from the city were awaiting him, and then he had no definite idea of what he intended to do.

She was dressed exactly as she had been on her previous visit, and she made obeisance almost to the floor, in greeting him, as she then had done.

He hastened her recovery from the deep curtsy by taking her hands and raising her to an upright posture.

"You have come to see me again? I am very glad to see you," he said, with eager politeness.

"Nakoda say you wish see me. Tha's why I come." There was not a trace of her former coquetry in her manner.

"Yes, I had to send Ido after you. I don't suppose you would ever have let me see you again if I had not."

She shrugged her shoulders imperceptibly. "Me you don' wish marrying with. You send me 'way. What I do?"

"We could be capital friends, even if we didn't care to marry, couldn't we?"

"Frien'? I don' wan' frien'," she returned, coldly.

"But I'd like to have you for my friend, all the same, though I'm afraid it's not possible. Ido"—he hesitated—"Ido says you're going to be married, you know."

She inclined her head.

"You're not married yet, are you?" he asked in alarm, forgetting that he had put this same question to the nakoda the day before.

"Nod yit."

"Do you—um—like him?"

"Which one, my lord?" She looked up at him innocently.

"Oh, both of them!" He was beginning to get angry. He would find pleasure in laying violent hands upon the two, one at a time.

"Jus' liddle bit, augustness."

"Better than you do me?" he demanded, jealously.

She shook her head decisively.

"You nod so ole, an' nod so—hairylike." She rubbed her little hands over her face, by which he understood that the two wore beards. They were doubtless of his own country. [8]

He hardly knew what to say next, and the silence grew embarrassing to him. She broke it by remarking, very quietly: "Nakoda inform me you wan' make liddle bit talk ad me."

He turned to the match-maker, who was pretending deep interest in a framed drawing on the wall. "Say, Ido, just step into the next room a minute, will you?"

He turned back to the girl, as soon as Ido had obeyed him, with extravagant alacrity.

"You have never even told me your name," he said.

"Yuki."

"That means 'Snowflake,' doesn't it? I like it. Well now, Yuki, mayn't I visit you at your home, before you are married?"

He was anxious to see what her people were like, and how she lived.

"Mos' poor house in all Tokyo—so liddle bit house augustness nod lige come."

"But I don't care if it is. I want to come anyhow. I want to see you, not the house. Won't you tell me where you live?"

She shook her head. "No," she said with simple directness, and then added as an afterthought, "House too small. You altogedder too big to enter thad liddle bit insignificant hovel."

Her answer gave him offense. He wondered why she should dissemble, wondered whether she was laughing at him. A glance at her, however, and his distrust vanished. She seemed such a simple little body, yet he knew he did not understand her.

Her eyes, which she had kept turned downward, slowly uplifted and looked questioningly into his own. Such wonderful eyes! Such a simple, exquisite face! He was suddenly suffused with a great wave of tenderness, and he bent low, and gently made prisoners of her hands. However indefinite his purpose had been up to this time, it was definite enough now.

"Do you remember, Yuki, what you asked me when you were here before?"

---

[8] Their having beards mark Yuki's two other suitors as Westerners since Japanese men were customarily clean-shaven.

"Yes." She still gazed at him questioningly.

"Would you like to—would you rather marry me than one of those other fellows?" he said, softly.

"Yes," again, in the smallest voice this time.

He hesitated, and she asked, quickly, "You *wan'* me do so?"

"That's just what I want, Yuki, dear," he whispered, drawing her hands to his lips.

"All ride." She trembled—perhaps shivered is the better word—as she said this, but gave no other sign of emotion.

Before Jack could so much as touch his lips to her forehead, Ido entered, smiling his professional blessing. It was evident that in the other room he had found no drawing to distract his attention, and a large new peephole in the immaculate shoji indicated where he had given all his eyes and ears to what was going on, and he could wait no longer to press his claim.

Jack, seeing an unpleasant duty before him, and desiring to have done with it at once, told Yuki that he would be back in a minute, and led the nakoda into the room out of which he had just come.

Ido immediately began to make terms. This part was loathsome to the young man.

"Why," he said, hotly, "if we're to be married, she can have all she wants and needs." That wouldn't do at all, the nakoda told him, warily. There would have to be a marriage settlement and a stated allowance agreed upon. He would have to pay more, also, as she was a maid and not a widow.

When the ugly terms of the agreement were completed, the nakoda bowed himself out, and Jack went back to Yuki. He found her changed; her simplicity had left her, and her coquetry had returned. She stood off from him, and he felt constrained and awkward. After a time she demanded of him, with a shrewd inflection in her voice:

"You goin' to lige me, excellency?"

"No question of that," he answered promptly, smiling.

"No," she repeated, "tha's sure thing," and then she laughed at her own assurance, and she was so pretty he wanted to kiss her, but she backed from him in mock alarm.

"Tha's nod ride," she declared, "till we marry."

"God speed the day!" he said, with devout joyousness. Still approaching her, as she backed [away] from him, he questioned her boyishly:

"And you? Will you like me?"

She surveyed him critically. Then she nodded emphatically. They laughed together this time, but when he approached her she grew fearful. He did not want to frighten her.

"You god nod anudder wife?" she asked.

"No! Good heavens!"

"I god nod anudder hosban'," she informed him, complacently.

"I should hope not."

"Perhaps," she said, "you marrying with girl in Japan thad god marry before. Me? I *never*."

"No, of course not." He didn't quite understand what she was driving at.

Then she said: "You pay more money ad liddle girl lige me whad nod been marry before?"

He recoiled and frowned heavily at her.

"I settled that matter with the nakoda," he said, coldly.

Seeing he was displeased, she tried to conciliate him. She smiled at him, engagingly, coaxingly.

"You don' lige me anymore whicheven."

But his face did not clear up. She had hurt him deeply by her reference to money.

"Perhaps you don' want me even," she suggested, tentatively. "I bedder go 'way. Leave you all 'one."

She turned and was making her way slowly out of the room, when he sprang impetuously after her.

"Don't, Yuki!" he cried, and caught her eagerly in his arms. She yielded herself to his embrace, though she was trembling like a little frightened child. For the first time he kissed her.

After she had left him, he stared with some wonder at the reflection of himself in a mirror. So he was to be married, was he? Yes, there was no getting out of it now. As for that, he didn't want to get out of it—of this he was quite sure. He was very well content—nay, he was enthusiastically happy with what the future promised.

But his happiness might have been felt in less measure if his eyes, instead of staring at his mirrored likeness, could have been fixed on Yuki.

She had borne herself with a joyous air to the jinrikisha, but once within it, and practically secure from observation, the life had seemingly gone out of her. The brown of her skin had paled to gray, and all the way to Tokyo her eyes shifted neither to right nor left, but stared straight ahead into nothingness, and once, when Ido looked down, he found that they were filled with tears.

V.

In Which the East and the West Are United

A few days later they were married. It was a very quiet little tea-drinking ceremony, and, unlike the usual Japanese wedding, there was not the painful crowd of relatives and friends attendant. In fact, no one was present, besides themselves, save Jack's man and maid and the nakoda, while Yuki herself sang the marriage song.

They started housekeeping in an ideal spot. Their house, a bit of art in itself, was built on the crest of a small hill. On all sides sloped and leaned green highlands, rich in foliage and warm in color. Beyond these smaller hillocks towered the jagged background of mountain-peaks, with the halo of the skies bathing them in an eternal glow. A lazy, babbling little stream dipped and threaded its way between the hillocks, mirroring on its shining surface the beauty of the neighboring hills and the inimitable landscapes pictured on the canvas of God—the skies—and seeing like a twisted rainbow of ever-changing and brilliant colors. But no surges disturbed its waters, even far beyond where it emptied into the mellow Bay of Tokyo.

From their elevation on the hill they could see below them the beautiful city of Tokyo, with its many-colored lights and intricate maze of streets. And all about them the hills, the meadows, the valleys, and forests bore eloquent testimony to the labor of the Color Queen.

Pink, white, and blushy-red twigs of cherry and plum blossoms, idly swaying, flung out their suave fragrance on the flattered breeze, the volatile handmaid of young May, who had freed all the imprisoned perfumes, unhindered by the cynical snarl of the jealous winter, and, with silent, persuasive wooing had taught the dewy-tinctured air to please all living nostrils. So from the glowing and thrilling thoughts that tremble on the young tree of life is love distilled, and, unmindful of the assembling of the baffled powers of cold caution and warning fear, the heart is filled with fountain tumults it cannot dissemble.

Jack Bigelow was fascinated and bewildered at the turn events had taken. He was very good and gentle to her, and for several days after the ceremony she seemed quite happy and contented. Then she disappeared, and for a week he saw nothing of her.

He greatly missed her—his little bride of three or four days. He longed ardently for her return, and her absence alarmed him. Her little arts and witcheries had grown on him even in this short period of their acquaintance.

Towards the end of the week she slipped into the house quietly, and went about her household duties as though nothing unusual had occurred. She did not offer to tell him where she had been, and he felt strangely unwilling to force her confidence.

Instead of becoming better acquainted with her, each day found him more puzzled and less capable of knowing or understanding her. Now she was clinging, artless, confiding, and again shrewd and elfish. Now she was laughing and singing and dancing as giddily as a little child, and again he could have sworn she had been weeping, though she would deny it stoutly, and pooh-pooh and laugh away such an idea.

He asked her one day how she would like to be dressed in American clothes. She mimicked him. She mimicked everything and everyone, from the warbling of the birds to the little man and maid who waited on them.

"I loog lige this," she said, and humped a bustle under her ridiculously tight omeshi and slipped his large sun hat over her face. Then she laughed out at him, and flung her arms tightly about his neck.

"You wan' me be American girl?"

"You are a witch, Yuki-san," he said.

"I wan' new dress," she returned, promptly, and held a pink little palm out. He frowned. He almost disliked her when she spoke of money. He filled her hands, however, with change from his pockets, and when she broke away from him, which she did as soon as she had obtained the money, he wanted to take it back. Her pretty laughter sifted out to him through the shoji at the other side, and he knew she was mocking him again.

"It is her natural love of dress and finery," he told himself. "It is the eternal feminine in her, and it is bewitching."

The next day, as she sat opposite to him, eating her infinitesimal bit of a breakfast—a plum, a small fish, and a tiny cup of tea—on a little black lacquer tray, he announced mysteriously that he was going "on business" to the city.

She desired to accompany him, as became a dutiful wife.

No, he told her, that was impossible. His mission was of a secret nature, which could not be divulged until his return.

Then she insisted that she would follow behind him after the manner of a slave; and when he laughed at her, she begged quite humbly and gently that he would condescend to honorably permit her to go with him, and then he was for telling her his whole pretty story, and the surprise he had concocted to please her, when she grew capricious and insisted that she would not stir one little bit of an inch from the house, and that he must go all alone to the city and attend to his great, magnificent business!

He went down to Tokyo, and in his boyish, blundering fashion he purchased silk and crêpe and linen sufficient for fifty gowns for her.

She thanked him extravagantly. She could not imagine what she would do with so much finery. Her honorable person was augustly insignificant, and could not accommodate so much merchandise.

"Now," he thought with inward satisfaction, "that ghost of a money question will be laid. She has everything she wants and shall have. I want to do for her, and give her things without being wheedled into it. It is that which irritates me."

But a few days later she came to him breathless and flustered. Lo! someone had stolen all the beautiful goods he had bought her. It was neither their man nor maid. No, no! that was altogether impossible! They were honest, simple folk, who feared the gods. But they were all quite gone—where she could not say. Who had taken them, she could not guess. Perhaps she, her unworthy self, and he, his honorable augustness, had been extremely wicked in their former state, and the gods were now punishing them in their present life. It would be wicked and unavailing to attempt to search for the missing goods. It was the will of the gods. Maybe the gods had been offended at such ruthless extravagance. Ah, yes, that was a better solution of the theft. Of course, the gods were angry. What gods would not be? It was sinful to buy so many things at once.

She affected great distress over the loss, and her husband, somewhat bewildered at her elaborate apologies for the thief who had stolen them, tried to comfort her by saying he would buy her double the quantity again, whereat she became very solemn.

"No, no," she said. "Bedder give me money to buy. I will purchase jus' liddle bit each time—to please the gods."

VI.

The Adventuress

THE man in the hammock was not asleep, for in spite of the lazy, lounging attitude, and the hat which hid the gray eyes beneath, he was very much awake, and keenly interested in a certain small individual who was sitting on a mat a short distance removed from him. He had invited her several times to reduce that distance, but up to the present she had paid no heed to his suggestions. She was amusing herself by blowing and squeezing between her lower lip and teeth the berry of the winter cherry, from which she had deftly extracted the pulp at the stem. She continued this strange occupation in obstinate indifference to the persuasive voice from the hammock.

"I say, Yuki, there's room for two in this hammock. Had it made on purpose."

She continued her cherry-blowing without so much as making a reply, though one of her blue eyes looked at him sideways, and then solemnly blinked.

"What's the matter, Yuki? Got the dumps again, eh?"

No reply.

"Look here, Mrs. Bigelow, I'll come over and elope forcibly with you if you don't obey me."

She dimpled scornfully.

"Ah, that's right! Smile, Yuki. You're so pretty, so bewitching, so irresistible when you smile."

Yuki nodded her head coolly.

"How you lige me smiling forever?" she suggested.

"That wouldn't do," he said, grinning at her from beneath his tipped hat. "That would be tiresome."

"Tha's why I don' smiling to-day."

"Why?"

"All yistidy I giggling."

He shouted with laughter at her.

"Move your mat here, Yuki," indicating a spot close to his hammock. "I want to talk to you."

"My ears are—"

"Too small to hear from that distance," finished her husband. "Come."

"Thangs," with great dignity, "I am quide comfor'ble. I don' wan' sit so near you, excellency."

"Why, pray?"

"Why? Hm! I un'erstan'. Tha's because I jus' your liddle bit slave."

"You're my wife, you little bit fraud."

"Wife? Oh, I dunno." She pretended to deliberate.

"Then you've tricked me into a false marriage, madam," declared her husband, with great wrath.

"Tha's fault nakoda."

"What is?"

"Thad you god me for wife, and," slowly, "servant."

"Fault! Come here, servant, then. Servants must obey."

"Nod so bad master, making such grade big noises," she laughed back daringly. "Besides, servant must sit long way off from thad same noisy master."

"And wife?"

"Oh, jus' liddle bit nearer." She edged perhaps half an inch closer to him. "Wife jus' liddle bit different from servant."

"Look here, Mrs. Bigelow, you're not living up to your end of the contract. You swore to honor and obey—"

She laughed mockingly.

"Yes, you did, madam!"

"I din nod. Tha's jus' ole Kirishitan marriage."

He sat up amazed.

"What do you know of the Christian marriage service?"

"Liddle bit."

"Come over here, Yuki."

"You like me sing ad you?"

"Come over here."

"How you like me danze?—liddle bit summer danze?"

"Come over here. What's a summer dance, anyhow?"

She ran lightly indoors, and was back so soon that she seemed scarcely to have left him. She had slipped on a red-and-yellow flimsy kimono, and had decked her hair and bosom with flaming poppies.

"Tha's summer sunshine," she said, spreading her garment out on each side with a joyous little twirl. "I am the Sun-goddess, and you?—you jus' the col', dark earth. I will descend and warm you with my sunshine." For a moment she stood still, her head thrown back, her face shining, her lips parted and smiling, showing the straight little white teeth within. Then she danced softly, ripplingly, back and forth. The summer winds were sighing and laughing with her. Her face shone out above her lightly swerving figure, her little hands and bare arms moved with inimitable grace.

"You are a genius," he said to her, when she had subsided, light as a feather blown to his feet.

"Tha's sure thing," she agreed, roguishly.

Her assurance in herself always tickled him immensely. He threw his hat at her with such good aim that it settled upon her head. She approved his clever shot, laughed at him and then, pulling it over her eyes, lay down on the mats and imitated his favorite attitude to a nicety. He laughed uproariously. He was in fine humor. They had been married over a month now, and she had not left him, save that first time. He was growing pretty sure of her now.

She perceived his good-humor, and immediately bethought herself to take advantage. She put the rim of his hat between her teeth, imitated a monkey, and crawled towards him, pretending to beg for her performance. He stretched his long arms out and tried to reach her, but she was far enough off to elude him.

"You godder pay," she said, "for thad nize entertainments I giving you."

He threw her a yen. She made a face. "That all?" she said, in a dreadfully disappointed voice, but, despite her acting, he saw the greedy eagerness of her eyes. All the good-humor vanished.

"Look here, Yuki," he said, with a disagreeable glint in his eyes, "you've had a trifle over fifty dollars this week. I don't begrudge you money, but I'll be hanged if I'm going to have you dragging it out of me on every occasion and upon every excuse you can make. You have no expenses. I can't see what you want with so much money, anyhow."

"I godder save," said Yuki, mysteriously, struck with this brilliant excuse for her extravagance.

"What for?"

"Why, same's everybody else. Some day I nod have lods money. Whad I goin' do then? Tha's bedder save, eh?"

"I've married you. I'll never let you want for anything."

"Oh, you jus' marry me for liddle bit while."

"You've a fine opinion of me, Yuki."

"Yes, fine opinion of you," she repeated after him.

"There's enough money deposited in a bank in Tokyo to last you as long as you live. If it's ever necessary for me to leave you for a time, you will not want for anything, Yuki."

"But," she said, argumentatively, "when you leaving me I henceforward a widder. I nod marry with you any longer. Therefore I kin nod take your money." This last with heroic pride.

"Boo! Your qualms of conscience about using my money are, to say the least, rather extraordinary."

"When you leaving me?" she commenced again.

"Why do you persist in that? I have no idea of leaving you."

"What!" She was quite frightened. "You goin' stay with me forever!" There was far more fear than joy in her voice.

"Why not?" he demanded, sharply, watching her with keen, savage eyes.

"My lord," she said, humbly, "I could nod hear of thad. It would be wrong. Too grade sacrifice for you honorable self."

He was not sure whether she was laughing at him or not.

"You needn't be alarmed," he said, gruffly. "I'm not likely to stay here forever." He turned his back on her.

Suddenly he felt her light little hand on his face. She was standing close by the hammock. He was still very angry and sulky with her. He closed his eyes and frowned. He knew just how she was looking; knew if he glanced at her he would relent ignominiously. She pried his eyes gently open with her fingers, and then kissed them, as softly as a tiny bird might have done. Gradually she crawled into the hammock with him, regardless of non-assistance.

"Augustness," she said, her arms about his neck now, though she was sitting up and leaning over him. "Listen ad me."

"I'm listening."

"Look ad me."

He looked, frowned, smiled, and then kissed her. She laughed under her breath, such a queer, triumphant, mocking small laugh. It made him frown again, but she kissed the frown into a smile once more. Then she sat up.

"Pray excuse me. I wan' sit ad your feet and talk ad you."

"Can't you talk here?" he demanded, jealously.

"Nod so well. I gittin' dazzled. Permit me," she coaxed. He released her grudgingly. She sat close to him on the floor. She sighed heavily, hypocritically.

"What is it now?"

"Well, you know I telling you about those moneys."

"Yes," he said, wearily. "Let's shut up on this money question. I'm sick of it."

"I lige make confession ad you."

"Well?"

"I god seventeen brudders and sisters!" she said, with slow and solemn emphasis.

"What!" He almost rolled out of the hammock in his amazement.

"Seventeen!" She nodded with ominous tragedy in her face and voice.

"Where do they live?"

"Alas! in so poor part of Tokyo."

"And your father and mother?"

"Alas! Also thad fadder an' mudder so ole lige this." She illustrated, bowing herself double and walking feebly across the floor, coughing weakly.

"Well?" he prompted sharply.

"I god take all thad money thad ole fadder an mudder an' those seventeen liddle brudders an sisters. Tha's all they god in all the whole worl'."

"But don't any of them work? Aren't any of them married? What's the matter with them all?"

"Alas! No. All of them too young to worg or marry, excellency."

"All of them too young?"

"Yes. Me—how ole I am? Oldes' of all! I am twenty-eight—no, thirty years ole," she declared, solemnly.

He nearly collapsed. He knew she was a mere child; knew, moreover, that she was lying to him. She had done so before.

"Even if you are thirty, I fail to see how you can have seventeen brothers and sisters younger than yourself."

She lost herself a moment. Then she said, triumphantly, "My fadder have two wives!"

He surveyed her in studious silence a moment. Her attitude of trouble and despair did not deceive him in the slightest. Nevertheless, he wanted to laugh outright at her, she was such a ridiculous fraud.

"Do you know what they'd call you in my country?" he said, gravely. She shook her head.

"An adventuress!"

"Ah, how *nize*," she sighed with envious blissfulness. "I wish I live ad your country—be adventuressesses."

"How much do you want now, Yuki?"

She pretended to calculate on his fingers.

"Twenty-five dollar," she announced.

He gave it to her, and she slipped it into the bosom of her kimono. He watched her curiously, wondering what she did with all the money she secured from him.

All of a sudden she put this question to him.

"Say, how much it taking go ad America?"

"How much? Oh, not much. Depends how you go. Four hundred, or five hundred dollars, possibly."

She groaned. "How much come ad Japan?"

"The same."

She sighed. "Sa-ay, kind augustness, I wan' go ad America. Pray, give me money go there."

"I'll take you some day, Yuki."

She retreated before this offer.

"Ah, thangs—yes, some day, of course." Then, after a meditative moment: "Sa-ay, it taking more money than thad three-four hunded dollar whicheven?"

"Yes; about that much again for incidentals—possibly more."

She sighed hugely this time, and he knew she was not affecting.

A few days later, poking among her pretty belongings, as he so much liked to do—she was out in the garden gathering flowers for their dinner table—he found her little jewel-box. Like everything else she possessed, it was daintily perfumed. At the top lay the few pieces of jewelry he had bought for her on different occasions when he had taken her on trips to the city. He lifted the top tray, and then he saw something that startled him. It was a roll of bank-bills. He took it out and counted it. There was not quite one hundred and fifty dollars. He calculated all he had given her. It amounted to a little over twice this sum. She had been saving, after all! What was her object?

And, his suspicions awakened by this discovery, he searched uneasily further through her apartments, and discovered, rolled like a huge piece of carpet and covered over by a large basket, the crêpe and silks she had protested were stolen.

VII.
My Wife!

THE second time his wife left him, Jack Bigelow was very wretched. He missed her exceedingly, though he would not have admitted it, for he was also very angry with her.

When she had gone away that first time, so soon after their marriage, he had not felt her absence as he did now, for then she had not become a necessity to him. But she had lived with him now two whole months, and had become a part of his life. She was not a mere passing fancy, and he knew it was folly to endeavor so to convince himself, as in his resentment at her treatment he was trying to do.

The house was desolate without her. Everywhere there were evidences of his little girl. Here a pair of her tiny sandals, some piece of tawdry kanzashi for her hair, her koto, samisen, and little drum; in the zashishi, in her own little room, and all over the house lingered the faint odor of her favorite perfume, so subtle it made the young man weak.

He grew to hate the silence of the rooms. Their household had always been small, with just a man and maid to wait on them; and now only one presence gone from it, and yet how painfully quiet the place had grown! He realized what all her little movements had become to him. He stayed outdoors as much as he could, only to return restlessly to the house, with a faint hope that perhaps she was hiding somewhere in it, and playing some prank on him, as she was fond of doing bursting out from some unexpected place of hiding. But there was no trace of her anywhere; and when the second day actually passed, the realization that she was indeed gone forced itself home to him, leaving him stupid with rage and despair.

He was bitterly angry with her. She had no right to leave him like this, without a word of explanation. How was he to know where she had gone or what might happen to her? And the thought of anything dire really overtaking her nearly drove him distracted. He hung around the balconies of the house, wandered down into the garden, and strayed restlessly about. And all the time he knew he was waiting for her, and in the waiting doubling his misery.

She came back in four days, slipped into the house noiselessly and ran up to her room. He heard her, knew she had returned, but checked his first impulse to go to her, and threw himself back on a couch, where he assumed a careless attitude, which he relentlessly changed to a stern, unapproachable, forbidding one.

Suddenly he heard her voice. It came floating down the stairs, every weird minor note thrilling, mocking, fascinating him. "Toko-ton-yare ron-ton-ton!" she sang. Then the voice ceased a moment. She was waiting for him to call her. He did not move. He was certainly very angry with her. He would not forgive her readily.

She began beating on her drum. He heard her making a great noise in the little room upstairs, and understood her object. She was trying to attract him. Suddenly she whirled down the stairs and burst in on him with a merry peal of laughter.

He ignored her sternly. She ceased her noise and laughter, and, approaching him, studied him with her head tilted bewitchingly on one side.

"You angery ad me, excellency?" she inquired with solicitude.

No reply.

"You very mad ad me, augustness?"

Still no reply.

"You very cross ad me, my lord?"

Jack regarded her in contemptuous silence.

She shouted now, a high, mocking joyous note in her laughter.

"Hah! You very, very, very, very *affended*, Mister Bigelow?"

"It seems to please you, apparently," said Jack, scathingly, wasting his sarcasm, and turning his eyes from her.

She laughed wickedly.

"Ah, tha's so nize."

"What is?" he demanded, sharply.

"Thad you loog so angery. My! You loog like grade big—whad you call thad?—toranadodo." She knew how to pronounce "tornado," but she wanted to make him laugh. She failed in her purpose, however. She tried another way.

"*How* you change!" She sighed with beatific delight.

Jack growled.

"Dear me! I thing you grown more nize-loogin," she said.

Jack got up and walked across to the window, turning his back deliberately on her, and whistling with forced gaiety, his hands in his pockets. She approached him with feigned timidity and stood at his elbow.

"You glad see me bag, excellency?"

"No!" shortly.

This emphatic answer frightened her. She was not so sure of herself, after all.

"You wan' me go 'way?" she asked, in the smallest voice.

"Yes."

She loitered only a moment, and then "Ah-bah" (good-bye), she said softly.

He felt, for he would not turn around to see, that she was crossing the room slowly, reluctantly. He heard the shoji pushed aside, and then shut to. He was alone! He sprang forward and called her name aloud. She came running back to him and plunged into his arms. He held her close, almost fiercely. The anger was all gone. His face was white and drawn. The dread of losing her again had overpowered him. When she tried to extricate herself from his arms, he would not let her go. He sat down on one of the chairs, and held her on his knee. She was laughing now, laughing and pouting at his white face.

"My crashes!" she cried. "You loog lige ole Chinese priest ad the temple." She pulled a long face, and drew her pretty eyes up high with her fingertips; then she chanted some solemn words, mocking mirthfully her ancestors' religion.

But her husband was grave. He had not the heart to find mirth even in her naughtiness.

"Yuki," he said, "you must be serious for a moment and listen to me."

"I listenin', Mr. Solemn-Angery-Patch!" She meant "Cross-patch." "You loog lige—"

"Where did you go?"

"Oh, jus' liddle bit visit."

"Where did you go?" he repeated, insistently.

"Sa-ay, I forgetting."

"Answer me."

She pretended to think, and then suddenly to remember, sighing hypocritically all the while.

"I lige forgitting," she said.

"Forgetting what?"

"Where I been."

"Why?"

"Tha's so sad. Alas! I visiting thad ole fadder an' mudder, ninety-nine and one hundred years ole, and those seventeen liddle brudders an' sisters. You missing me very much?" she changed from the subject of her whereabouts.

"No!" he said, shortly, stung by her falsity.

"I don' thing so!"

"Where were you, Yuki?"

"Now, whad you wan' know for, sinze you don' like me whicheven?"

"Did I say so?"

"You say you don' miss."

"I lied," he said, bitterly. "Where were you?"

"Jus' over cross street, see my ole friend ad tea-garden."

"I thought you said you were visiting your people?"

She was not at all abashed.

"Sa-ay, firs' you saying you miss me; then thad you lie. Sa-ay, you big lie, I jus' liddle bit lie."

"Yuki, listen to me. If you leave me like this again you need never come back. Do you understand?"

"Never?"

"I mean that."

"Whad you goin' do? Git you 'nudder wife?"

He pushed her from him in savage disgust. She laughed with infinite relish.

He sat down a little distance from her, and put his face wearily between his hands. Yuki regarded him a moment, and then she silently went to him, pulled his hands down, and kissed his lips.

"I have missed you terribly," he said, hoarsely.

She was all compunction.

"I very sawry. I din' know you caring very much for poor liddle me, an' p'raps I bedder nod come bag ad you."

"Why did you come, then?" he asked, gently.

"I coon' help myself," she said, forlornly. "My feet aching run bag ad you, my eyes ill to see you, my hands gone mad to touch you."

She had grown, in a moment, serious, but also melancholy.

After a pause she said, more brightly, "I bringin' you something—something so nize, dear my lord."

"What is it, Yuki, dear?" He was reluctant to let her go even for a moment.

"Flowers," she said—"summer flowers."

He released her, and she brought them to him, a huge bunch of azaleas. She buried her delightful little nose in them. "Ah," she said, "flowers mos' sweetes' thing in all the worl', an' all them same flowers for you, for you."

"Where did you get them, dear?" he asked, taking her hands instead of the flowers, and drawing her, flowers and all, into his arms. She faltered a little, and then said, with the old daring smile flashing back in her face: "Nize Japanese gents making me present those flowers."

He caught her wrists in a grip of iron. "What do you mean?" he demanded, fiercely, wild jealousy assailing him.

She pulled herself from him, and regarded the little wrists ruefully.

"Ain' you shamed?" she accused.

"Yes!" He kissed the little wrists with an inward sob. "Tell me all, my little one. Please do not hide anything from me. I can't bear it."

"Thad Japanese gent wanter marry with me," she informed him, calmly smiling, and dimpling as if it amused her, and then making a face to show him her feelings in the matter.

"My! How he *adore* me!" she added, vividly.

"Marry with you! What do you mean? You are my wife."

"Yes, bud *he* din' know thad," she said, consolingly; "an' see, I bring his same flowers unto you."

He took them from her arms. They were all crushed now, and it distressed her. No Japanese can bear to see a flower abused. She fingered some of the petals sadly; then she sighed, looking up at him with tears in her eyes.

"Tha's mos' beautiful thing' in all the whole worl'," she said, indicating the flowers—"so pure, so kind, so sweet."

"I know something more beautiful and sweet, and—and pure."

"Ah, whad?" She said, her face shining, the pupils of the blue eyes so large as to make them look almost black.

"My wife!" he breathed.

VIII.
Yuki's Home

EVERY day, all unknown to Yuki, her husband looked in her little jewel-box. The pile of bills grew larger. He no longer refused her requests for money. The fund was quite large now. The last time he had counted it there was four hundred dollars. He took a whim[9] to make it five hundred, and that same day gave her a clear hundred dollars.

She had given him a solemn promise never to leave him again without his knowledge and consent, and for a whole month she had kept stead-fastly at home. It was the happiest month in his life, a month that spelled naught else but joy and sunshine.

But the day after he had given her the hundred dollars she came to him and begged very humbly to be permitted to visit her old father and mother and seventeen little brothers and sisters. She still kept up this deception. He refused her almost gruffly. He had grown selfish and spoiled under her care. All the day, however, he watched her suspiciously, fearful lest she should slip away. And he was right. In the evening, when she had left him for a moment, he saw her leaving the house. He took his hat, and, keeping at a good distance from her, but never losing sight of her for a moment, he followed her.

Twilight was falling. Softly, tenderly, the darkness swept away the ex-quisite rays of red and yellow that the departing sun had left behind, for it was crossing the waters, until, far in the distance, it dipped deep down as though swallowed up by the bay.

Yuki was walking rapidly towards Tokyo. It was only a short distance, but nevertheless the thought of her little tender feet treading it alone, and at such an hour, unnerved her husband.

Whatever her mission, wherever she was going, he would follow her. She belonged to him completely. She should never escape him now, he told himself.

She seemed to know her way, and showed no hesitation or fear when once in Tokyo, but bent her steps quickly and with assurance, until finally

---

[9] That is, he acted on a whim.

they were before the great terminal station at Shimbashi. They had now come a long distance. The girl looked tired; weary shadows were under her eyes, as she passed into the railway enclosure and bought a ticket for a town suburb a short distance from Tokyo.

Her husband went to the window, inquired where the girl was going, and bought a ticket for the same place.

Then began the long journey in the uncomfortable train, where there were no sleeping accommodations whatever. Yuki found a seat, and sat very quietly staring out at the flying darkness. After a time she put her head back against the seat and, despite the jolting of the train, fell asleep.

Her husband was close to her now—in the next seat, in fact. He could have touched her, as he so longed to do, but would not for fear of disturbing or frightening her.

When they reached the little town, the banging of the doors, the blowing of whistles, and shouts of the conductor awakened her. She came to life with a start, gathered her little belongings together, and left the train, her husband still following her.

It was a refined and beautiful little town they had arrived at, apparently the home of the exclusive and cultivated Japanese. Its atmosphere was grateful and pleasing after the crowded city of Tokyo, with its endless labyrinth of narrow streets and grotesque signboards and ceaseless noises.

Yuki had not far to walk. Only a few steps from the little station, and then she was before one of those old-fashioned, pretentious palaces once affected by the nobles. There were signs of neglect about the house and gardens, which had fallen out of repair. No coolies or servants were in sight. At the garden gate Yuki paused a moment, leaning wearily against it, ere she opened and passed through, up the garden walk, and disappeared into the shadows of the palace.

Her husband stood for a long time as though rooted to the spot. Then very slowly he retraced his steps to the railway station, bought his ticket, and returned to Tokyo. He felt sure she would come back to him.

And she did, hardly two days later. He was very gentle to her this time. There were no more questions asked, and she vouchsafed no explanation.

But she came back to him strangely docile and submissive. All the old mockery and folly had vanished. She was angelic in her sweet tenderness and solicitude. But once he found her in tears. She protested they had come there because she had laughed so hard. Another time, when he offered her money, she refused passionately to accept it. It was the first time since she had lived with him. Thereafter she refused to take even the regular weekly allowance agreed upon. He looked in her little jewel-box, and found the money all gone.

Her docility and gentleness strengthened his confidence in her. He was sure she would never leave him again. He even told her of this belief, and she did not deny it. But her eyes were tearful. With boyish insistence he teased her.

"Tell me so—that you will never leave me again."

"Never?" she said, but the word slipped from her lips as a question.

"Repeat it after me," he demanded. "Say: "I—shall—never—never— leave you again."

"Ah, you makin' fun ad me," she protested, begging the question.

But he still persisted, and made her repeat slowly after him, word by word, that she would remain with him till death should part them.

One day he found her laboriously occupied at her small writing-desk. Her little hand flew down the page, rapidly drawing the strange characters of her country's letters.

"What are you doing? You look as wise and solemn as a female Buddha."

Yuki carefully blotted and covered her letter. She did not answer him. Instead she held up her little stained fingers, to show him the ink on them. He sat down beside her, kissing the tips of her fingers.

"To whom were you writing, fairy-sage?" he said.

"To whom? My brudder."

"Your brother! Ah, you have a brother, have you? And where is he?"

She still hesitated, and he watched her keenly.

"He live ad Japan," she said, after a long moment.

"Japan is quite a big place," remarked her husband, suggestively. "He has rather large quarters for one fellow, don't you think?"

"Japan liddle bit country," she argued, trying to change the subject. "America, perhaps, grade big place, big as half the whole worl'—"

"Not quite," interposed her husband, smiling.

"Well, big's one-quarter of the worl', anyhow," she declared. "Bud Japan! Mos' liddle bit insignificant spot on all the beautiful maps."

"What part of Japan does your family live in?"

"Liddle bit town two hunded miles north of Tokyo."

"Indeed."

She had spoken the truth, he knew.

"Why doesn't your brother come to see you?"

Now that he had commenced it, he stuck to his catechism doggedly.

"He don' know where I live," she said.

"Don't know! That's strange. Why doesn't he?"

"I 'fraid tellin'."

"Afraid of what?"

"Afraid he disowning me forever."

"Why should he do that?"

He was getting interested. He disliked wringing her secrets from her in this wise. He wanted her confidence unsolicited; but his curiosity had the better of him. "Why should he disown you?" he repeated.

"Because I marrying—" she paused, somewhat piteously, holding one of his hands closely between her own small ones, and entreatingly pressing it as though begging him not to pursue his questions.

"Well?" he said—"because you married—"

"You," she finished.

"Oh!" His ejaculation was rueful. Then he laughed, and squared his shoulders, and shook his finger at her.

"What's the matter with me? Am I not good enough?"

"Too honorably good," she declared, humbly.

"Then why does your family object to receiving me into its bosom, eh?"

"Because you jus' barbarian," she said apologetically, and then swiftly tried to make amends. "Barbarian mos' nize of all. Also *I* am liddle bit barbarian. I god them same barbarous eyes an' oogly hair—"

"Loveliest hair in the world," he said, stroking it fondly. "But never mind, dearie. Don't look so distressed. It's not your fault, of course, that your people disapprove of me."

"They don' disprove," she interrupted him, her distress deepening. "They don' never seen you even."

"But I thought you said—"

"I jus' guess. Tha's why I don' tell thad brudder. Mebbe he dis'prove you when he see you grade big barbarian. Tha's bedder nod tell unto him."

"But where does he think you are all the time?"

"He?" She lost her head a moment. "Likewise," she continued, "he also travel from home. Perhaps he also marrying with beautiful barbarian leddy. Tha's whad I dunno."

"I don't quite understand," said her husband. "But never mind. If you don't like the subject, and it's plain you don't, you sha'n't be bothered with it."

"Thangs," she said, gratefully.

On another day, as she sat opening his American mail with her small paper-knife, a picture of a young American girl fell from the envelope.

Yuki picked it up, and regarded it with dilated eyes and lips that quivered. It was the first shock of jealousy she had experienced. One of his own countrywomen, then, must love him. No Japanese girl would send her picture to any man, save her lover.

Her first impulse was to tear the picture across. She did not want him to see it. Perhaps even the pictured face might win him back, she thought jealously. But she did not destroy it. She hid it in the sleeve of her kimono, and for a whole week she tortured herself with drawing it forth from its hiding-place and studying the face whenever she was alone a moment, comparing it with her own exquisite one in her small mirror.

Then conscience, or perhaps natural feminine curiosity to know who her rival was, prompted her to make humble confession to her husband of her theft.

He took the matter gaily, and seemed exuberantly happy at the idea of her being jealous, for she could not well hide this fact from him. He gloated over this apparent evidence of her love for him.

"Isn't she lovely?" he asked, enthusiastically, pointing to the picture, and then pretending to hug it to him.

"No," said Yuki, proudly. "Mos' oogly girl in all the whole worl'. Soach silliest things on her haed. I don' keer tha's hat or nod. Flowers, birds, beas', perhaps, an' rollin' her eyes this-a-way—"

"This is my sister," said Jack, gravely. "I am sorry you don't like her, Yuki. She'd just the sort of girl to love you."

Her little spurt of temper flickered out pitifully.

"Ah, *pray* forgive me," she implored. "I mos' silliest *mousmè* in all Japan. She jus' *lovely*, mos' sweet beautiful girl in all the whole worl'. Jus' like you, my lord."

IX.

The Mikado's Birthday

THE mellow summer was gone. With the dawn of the autumn the languor of the country seemed to increase. Now that the weather was cooler, however, they made frequent trips to the city, visiting the chrysanthemum shows, loitering through Ueno Park, the Shiba temples, and bazaars. And one day Jack shook gaily before her eyes a really awe-inspiring document. It was, in fact, an invitation, written in fine French, from a Japanese person of high rank, inviting him to attend a very important function, which was to be given at the Hôtel Imperial on the Mikado's birthday, which function was to be honored by the presence of "les princes et les princesses."

"We are going, of course," he told her. "It will be a change, and, besides, I want to show you off to my friends. There'll be hosts of them there, you know."

But she protested. First she set forth as excuse the fact that she was only an honorably rude and insignificant humble geisha girl, who would be out of place in so great and extraordinary an assemblage.

Then her husband quite seriously reproved her, and reminded her forcibly that she was anything but an insignificant geisha girl. She was, in fact, a very important person—his wife.

Ah, yes, she admitted that she had indeed grown in caste since her marriage with him; nevertheless, they had lived so honorably secluded together that she had forgotten all the polite mannerisms of society, which she had never been acquainted with at all, being only a crude girl of humble parentage. She would surely disgrace not only both of them by her behavior, but doubtless the whole assemblage. She would not know how to act, how to look, and when to speak.

Then Jack insisted, with affected selfishness, that she should look at and speak to no one but himself He would commit hari-kari, or joshi or any old kind of Japanese suicide, otherwise. And as for her manners, they were lovely, perfect, just right.

"Ah, bud you—" she deprecated. "You don' understan', you big barbarian. Those same honorable monsters, Japanese princes; whad, before all the gods, they goin' to thing of me?"

"That you are absolutely adorable. How could they help thinking so, unless they are stone blind. Besides, this isn't a Japanese affair at all. It's at a European hotel, and there'll be all sorts and conditions of people there. I was lucky to get the invitations. They aren't for everyone, you know. This is a big thing."

"*You* so big," she said, proudly.

"Well, no. It had really nothing to do with my size. You see, I have a half-Jap friend in America, and of course it's through him I'm favored."

"Ah, thad half-Jap, he was very high-up man ad Japan, perhaps?"

"Well, he was connected with some of the big families, though he was quite poor."

"Thad," said Yuki, with sudden vehemence, "is no madder ad Japan. Money! Who has thad money? Nod the ole families, the flower of the country, jus' the shop-keepers and the politicians."

Her husband was startled at her outbreak. He was astonished at her knowledge of existing conditions in her country. But she did not pursue the subject, saying she disliked it.

And the ball? What about that?

Well, she would not go with him. He must go to that all alone, for the million big reasons she had given him. Moreover, all the ladies would wear Parisian toilettes. It would be a disgrace for his wife to go in a kimono.

Again he was astonished at her. How did she know that on such occasions the ladies, Japanese included, dressed in European gowns?

Apparently she knew more concerning such matters than he had imagined. It was becoming plainer to him every day that his wife was of no ordinary family. And then the memory of the old rambling palace, doubtless her home, in the exquisite, aristocratic little town where he had followed her, supported this idea. Who was his wife, after all? Who were her people, and why had none of them come near her during all these months? What was the meaning of the mystery in which she had surrounded herself ever since he had known her. And now, when there was scarcely a doubt left in his mind of her love for him, why had he failed to win her confidence?

"I want to know just who you are, my little wife," he suddenly said. "I do not believe that tale about your people. I know you are not a geisha girl. You are not, are you?"

"No," she said, very softly.

"Then tell me. Who are your people? It is only right I should know this."

She looked up at him with intense seriousness. Then her eyes fluttered, and she went rambling into one of her fairy tales of nonsense.

"My people? Who they are? My august ancestors came from the moon. My one hundred grade-grandfathers fight and fight and fight like the lion, and conquer one-half of all Japan—fight the shogun, fight the ka-zoku, fight each other.[10] They were great Samourai, cutting off the haeds of aevery humble mans they don' like. So much bloodshed displeased the gods. They punishing all my ancestors, bringin' them down to thad same poverty of those honorable peebles killed by them. Then much distress an' sadness come forever ad our house. All pride, all haughty boasting, daed forever. Aeverybody goin' 'bout weepin' like ad a funeral. Nobody habby. What they goin' do git bag thad power an' reeches ag'in? Also one an-cestor have grade big family to keep from starving, an' one daughter beau-tiful as the moon of her ancestors. He weep more than all the rest of those ancestors, weep an' weep till he go blind like an owl ad day-time. Then the gods begin feel sawry. One of them mos' sawry of all. He also is de-scendant, of the Sun. Well, thad Sun-god he comin' down ad Japan, make big raddle an' noise, an' marrying with thad same beautifullest daughter of thad ole blind ancestor. Thad Sun-god my fadder. Me? I am the half-Moon-half-Sun offspring."

She had promised to accompany him, at all events, to see the review from the American legation tent, but at the last moment she backed out. She had seen it many times before, she declared. She was tired of it.

At first he swore he would not go without her. Why, the "show," he de-clared, would be nothing to him without her to see it with him. Half the pleasure—nay, all of it—would be gone. He was really keenly disap-pointed, but she coaxed and wheedled and petted around him, till, before he knew that he was aggrieved at her backsliding, he was well on his way.

The streets were thronged with a motley crowd of people. Jinrikishas were scurrying hither and thither, and little bits of humanity, in the shape of small men, small women, small children, and small dogs and cats, were colliding and jostling against the many ramshackle vehicles in the road. Gay flags and bunting were displayed everywhere, and the town presented a gala appearance.

---

[10] The shogun was the emperor's top military officer and the effective ruler of feudal Japan for seven centuries. The emperor's role was more symbolic. In the Tokugawa era (1603–1867), the shogunate was particularly strong. In 1868, the shogunate was abolished, and the mikado was restored as the governing ruler, as well as titular head, of the country.

Jack got out of his jinrikisha and pushed his way through the crowd until he came up to the parade-grounds. He found his way to the proper tent, and, with a half-score of former acquaintances about him, he was soon drawn into the babble and gush of small talk and jokes that tourists meeting each other in foreign lands usually indulge in.

Once on the parade-grounds, where infantry, cavalry, and artillery were forming themselves, it seemed as if he had suddenly left Japan altogether, and was once more in the modern Western world, of which he had always been a part.

There was nothing Oriental in this brave display of the imperial army. There was nothing Oriental in this bustling, noisy crowd of foreigners, each trying to outdo the other in importance and precedence. Only the skies and the little winds, and, in the distance, the sinuous outlines of the mountains and forests beyond, and the disks on the national flag displayed everywhere, were Japanese. And after his long seclusion in the country, the glitter dazzled him.

There were seven thousand men in the field, and the Mikado, surrounded by his generals, body-guard, outriders, and standard-bearers, reviewed the troops; and then, amid a great flourish, and hoarse cheering drowning the national hymn, which was being played by all the bands at once, he left the grounds.

Jack did not return after the parade to his home, much as he would have liked to do so. Some acquaintances who had crossed on the same steamer with him on his way to Japan carried him off triumphantly to their hotel, and that night he went with them to the imperial ball.

It was very late when he went home to Yuki. There was a faint light burning in the zashishi, and he wondered with some concern whether she were sitting up waiting for him. He did not see her at first when he entered the room, for the light of the andon had fluttered down dimly, and it was more the grayness of the approaching dawn which saved the room from complete darkness. Crossing the room, he came upon her. She had fallen asleep on the floor. She was lying on her back, her arms encircling her head. He was suddenly struck with her extreme youth. She seemed little more than a tired child, who had grown weary and had fallen asleep among her toys, for beside her on a tiny foot-high table was the little supper she had prepared for him, and which was now quite cold. On the other side of her were her tiny drum and samisen, with which she had been attempting doubtless to pass the evening by pulling from the strings some of that weird music he knew so well now.

For a long time her husband looked at her, and a feeling of intense isolation about her came over and suddenly possessed him. Why had he never been able to bridge that strange distance which lay like a pall between them, the feeling always that she was not wholly his own, that she had been but a guest within his house, a tiny wild bird that he had caught in some strange way and caged—caught, though she had come to him, as it were, for protection? Just as, when a boy, he remembered how a robin had beaten at his shutters, and he had saved it from an enemy, and afterwards how he had caged it, and how it had pined for its freedom.

The thought that he might yet lose Yuki caused him such anguish of mind it almost stunned him. He knelt down beside her, and drew her up in his arms, and then, as gently as a mother would have done, he carried her up the queer spiral stairway which led to their little upstairs room.

The next day she questioned him anxiously. Were there many ladies more beautiful than she at the ball? Had he enjoyed himself largely with them, and how could he live away hereafter from such mirth and gaiety? Why had he come back to little, insignificant her?

And he told her that never in all his life before had he longed so ardently for anyone as he had for her that previous night. That the day had been endless; the noise and show, the brassy merriment and cheer, were abhorrent to him, for she had not been there to rob it of its vulgarity with the charm of her sweet presence. That he had been rude in his efforts to escape it, had bullied the jinrikimen because they had seemed to creep, and that happiness and peace had only come back to him again when he had crossed his own threshold and had taken her in his arms.

Still, the wistful distress in her misty eyes was only in part dispelled.

"Last night," she said, "I broke my liddle jade bracelet. It is a bad omen."

"I will buy you a dozen new ones," he said.

"One million dozens cannot mend jus' thad liddle one," she returned, sadly, shaking her head. "It is a bad omen. Mebbe a warning from the gods."

Of what did they warn her? That she could not say, but she had heard that such an accident usually preceded the sorrows of love. Perhaps he would soon pass away from her, and, like the ghost of the fisher-boy Urashima,[11] who had left his fairy bride to return to his people, he too would pass out of her life, back into that from which he had come.

---

[11] According to Japanese legend, Urashima falls in love with and marries the daughter of the sea-dragon king, but eventually leaves her to return to human society and land.

X.

A Bad Omen

It was late in November. The parks were dropping their autumn glories and taking on the browner hues and hints of hoar-frost, black-and-white vestments, the sackcloth and ashes of winter. The recessional of the birds was dying away into silence. Soon the final, long-drawn amen of the north-wind would be breathed out over the deserted woods, where the anthem of praise had rung out to the worshipping air all through the golden days and silver nights of summer.

The still beauty of the autumn evening was piercingly melancholy, and, even with a loving sunset still lingering in the skies, a silken, gentle rain was falling, as though the gods were weeping over the death of the autumn, were weeping hopeless tears—the most tragic of all. The little house that stood alone on the hill faced to the west its wet roofs and shingles sparkling and glistening in the rays of the dying sunset that enveloped it.

Yuki opened a shoji (sliding paper door) of her chamber, and looked out wistfully at the city of Tokyo, that in the autumn silence was shining out like a gem, with its many strange lights and colors. She stole softly out on to a small balcony, and stepped down into the tiny garden as the night began to spread its mantle of darkness. A few minutes later her husband called to her:

"Yuki! Yuki!"

He drew her into the room, and closed the shoji behind her.

"You have been crying again!" he said, sharply, and turned her face up to the light.

"It is the rain on my face, my lord," she answered in the smallest voice.

"But you mustn't go out in the rain. You are quite wet, dear."

"Soach a little, gentle rain," she said. "It will not hurt jus' me. I loogin' aeverywhere 'bout for our liddle bit poor nightingale. Gone! Perhaps daed! Aeverything dies—bird, flowers, mebbe me!"

He put his hand over her mouth with a hurt exclamation.

"Don't!" he only said.

The maid brought in their supper on a tray, but before she could set it down Yuki had impetuously crossed the room and taken it from her hands.

"Go, go, honorable maid," she said. "I will with my own hands attend my lord's honorable appetite."

She knelt at his feet, geisha fashion, holding the tray and waiting for him to eat, but he took it from her gravely, and put it on the small table beside them, and then silently, tenderly, he took her small hands in his own.

"What is troubling you, Yuki? You must tell me. You are hiding something from me. What has become of my little mocking-bird? I cannot live without it."

"You also los' liddle bird?" she queried, softly—"jus' lige unto my same liddle nightingale?"

"I have lost—I am losing you," he said, suddenly, with a burst of anguish. "I cannot make you out these last few weeks. What has come over you? I miss your laughing and your singing. You are always sad now; your eyes—ah, I cannot bear it." His voice went suddenly anxious. "Tell me, is it—do you—want—need some more money, Yuki? You know you can have all you want."

She sprang to her feet fiercely.

"No, no, no, no!" she cried; "naever any more for all my life long, *dear* my lord."

"Then why—"

"Ah, *pray* don' ask why."

"But why—"

"Then listen unto me. I nod any longer thad liddle bit geisha girl you marrying with. I change grade big moach. Now you see me, I am one wooman, mebbe like wooman one hundred years ole—wise—sad—I change!"

"Yes," he said. "You are changed. You are my Undine,[12] and I have found your soul at last!"

One oppressive afternoon, when a nagging, bleating wind outdoors had prevented their going on their customary ramble through the woods or on a little trip to the city, Jack had fallen asleep. Long before he had awakened he had felt her warm, soothing presence near him, but with the pleasure it afforded him was mingled a premonition of disaster and a dread of something unhappy about her. He awoke to find her standing by him, her face, white and drawn, with a despair he could not comprehend.

---

[12] The mermaid Undine gained her soul by marrying a fisherman and bearing his child.

"What is it?" He started up fearfully. "Your eyes are tragic! You look as if you were contemplating something frightful."

She sank down to his feet, and, despite his protests, knelt and clung to him there, sobbing with passionate abandon.

"Don't! Don't! I can't bear you to do that. What is it, Yuki?"

"Oh, for liddle while, jus' liddle bit while, bear with me," she said.

"Little while! What do you mean?" he demanded.

She tried to regain her composure. Her laughter was piteous.

"I only liddle bit skeered," she said. "I—" she stammered—"I skeered 'bout thad liddle foolish jade bracelet, all smashed and broken."

"Is that all?"

"It is soach a bad omen! The gods trying to separate us, mebbe."

"Separate us?" His suspicions were growing. "How can they do that? It lies between you and me, such a—such a fate. The gods—ah, you are talking nonsense."

"The gods see inside," she said.

"Inside what?"

"Our hearts." Her voice was barely above a whisper.

"And what can they find there to distress you?" he asked, almost fiercely. She was hurting him with her failure to confide in him.

"The bracelet—" she began. "It is broken, an' love, too, mus' die—an' break!"

From that day her melancholy grew rather than diminished. But she had roused her husband's suspicions, and, her morbidness irritated rather than appealed to him. He felt that in some way he was being deceived. The day that he found her wardrobe neatly and carefully folded away in her queer little packing-case, as though in preparation for a journey, the full sense of her deceit dawned upon him. Hitherto when she had left him she had taken none of her belongings with her. He perceived it was now her intention to desert him utterly. He had served her purpose, apparently, and she was through with him.

His wrath burst its bounds. He had not known the capabilities of his angry passion. He tore the silken garments from the box with the fierce madness of one demented, then he pushed her into the room, and showed her where they lay scattered.

"The meaning of this?" he demanded, white to the lips with the intensity of his passion.

She remained mute. She did not even trouble to mock or laugh at him, nor would she weep. She seemed dazed and bewildered, and he, infuriated against her, said things which rankled in his conscience for years afterwards.

"Does a promise mean nothing to you—a promise—an oath itself? Were you, parrot-like, merely echoing my words when you swore to stay by me until—" his voice broke—"death?"

Still she made him no denial, and her silence maddened him, and drove him on with his bitter arraignment.

"What your object has been I fail to see, but you cannot deny that you have laid yourself out, have used every effort, every art and wile, of which you are mistress, to make me believe in you. And I—I—like a blind, deluded fool—ah, Yuki—there is something wrong, some hideous mistake somewhere. You have some secret, some trouble. Be frank with me. Can't you see—understand how I—I am suffering?"

She roused herself with an effort, but her words were pitifully conventional. She apologized for the trouble and noise she had brought into his house.

"You have not answered me!" he cried. "What was your intention? Did you intend to leave me? You shall answer me that!"

"It was bedder so," she said, and her voice fainted. She could speak no further.

"Then such was your intention!" He could hardly believe her words.

XI.

The Nightingale

WHEN Love lives after Trust is dead, then peace is an unknown quantity. A constraint that was baffling in its intense hopelessness now hedged up between these two. Yuki grew thin and wistful. Her whole attitude became one of pitiful attempted conciliation and humility, which with bitter suspicion her husband took to be confusion and guilt. Had she even affected somewhat of her old lightheartedness and attempted to win his forgiveness by her old audacious wiles, her husband would have forgotten and forgiven everything, glad of an excuse to renew the old close comradeship with her. But she made no such attempt.

She had acquired a peculiar fear of her husband, and unconsciously shrank from him, as though dreading to bring down on herself his further displeasure. She kept away from him as much as she could, though at times she made spasmodic, frantic efforts to assume her old lightheartedness, but these efforts were usually followed by passionate outbursts of tears, when she had drawn the shoji between them, and was once more alone with her own inward thoughts, whatever they were.

Meanwhile her husband kept the watch of a jailer over her. He was convinced that she was waiting for a chance to leave him, and this he was determined to frustrate. She had raised in him a feeling of the intensest bitterness, which amounted almost to antagonism towards her. And still beneath all this resentment and bitterness a tenderness and yearning for her threatened to strangle and overpower all other feeling. Her apparent fear of him hurt him terribly, and caused him distractedly at times to question whether he had been as kind to her as he might have been. Then his mind would inevitably revert to the fact that she was planning to leave him and his resentment would burn fiercer than ever.

By a common dread of the subject, both of them avoided alluding to it, and for this reason it weighed the heavier on their minds. He feared that any explanation she might attempt to make to him would only be some excuse put forward to reconcile him, and will his consent, to the impossible situation which he instinctively knew she intended to consummate.

She, on the other hand, watched wildly to turn the subject, dreading his wrath, which she was conscious was righteous.

To add to the gloom of their strained relations, a season of drizzly wet weather set in, which confined them to the house, and, moreover, Yuki was grieving and pining over the loss of a favorite nightingale that had made its home in the tall bamboo out in the midnight garden of their little home. Jack was misanthropic and cynical, restless as it is possible for a man to be under such galling circumstances, yearning nevertheless for things to be as they had been between him and his wife.

One night, at dusk, after an exceptionally sad and chilly meal indoors, Jack had come out alone, and was trying to soothe his senses with a fragrant cigar. Instinctively he was waiting for his wife. He missed her if she was absent from his side but a moment. Suddenly out of the gloaming soared out one long, thrilling note of sheer ecstasy and bliss, that quivered and quavered a moment, and then floated away into the maddest peals of melody, ending in a sob that was excruciating in its intense humanness. The nightingale had returned!

He sprang to his feet, and, trembling by the veranda rail, stared outward into the darkness. And then? Yuki came out from the shadows of their garden, and under the light of the moon, beneath their small balcony, she looked up into his eyes, and murmured in a voice thrilled by an inward sob, so timid and meek, so beseeching and prayerful:

"I lige please you, my lord!"

"The nightingale!" he whispered, with hoarse emotion. "Did you hear it? It has returned!"

"Nay, my lord—tha's jus' me! I jus' a liddle echo!"

She had learned the voice of the nightingale.

With an exclamation of indescribable tenderness he drew her into his arms, and for a few moments at least all the misery and pain and constraint of the last few weeks between them passed away and gave place to all their pent-up love and loneliness.

As he held her close to him, he was conscious at first only of the fact that she loved him, that she was clinging to him with somewhat of her old abandon, and then he felt her hands upon his arms. He could almost see them shaking and trembling. She was attempting to release herself! Struggling to be free! All of a sudden he released her, and stood breathing hard, his arms folded across his breast, waiting for her to do or say something to him.

She did not move. She stood before him, with her head down; and then her blue eyes lifted, and timidly, appealingly, they beseeched his own. She

"The Nightingale Song." From A Japanese Nightingale by Onoto Watanna (New York: Harper and Bros., 1901). Illustrated by Genjiro Yeto.

started to speak, stammered only a few incoherent words, and then, with a half-sob, she unsteadily crossed the room and left him alone.

Two days later, upon their household gloom came word from Taro Burton, announcing that he had arrived in Tokyo. Jack rushed off to meet him, telling Yuki he expected an old friend, and would bring him home that evening.

XII.

Taro Burton

Iᴛ may be that Jack Bigelow first awoke to the fact that for months he had been literally living in a dream-world when he saw his old college-chum, Taro Burton—the same dear, old, grave Taro! He rushed up to him in the old boyish fashion, wringing his hands with unaffected delight.

The past dream-months rolled for the moment from his memory, and Jack was once again the happy up-to-date American boy.

Taro had been delayed in America, he now told the other frankly, on account of the failure of his people to send him passage money until about a month ago. He had a few hardships to recount and some messages to deliver from mutual friends, and then he wanted to know all about Jack. Why had he failed to visit his people as promised? How much of the country had he seen? Why were his letters so few and far between?

Jack Bigelow laughed shortly. "Burton, old man," he said, "I've been dead to everything in Japan—in the world, in fact—save one entrancing subject."

"Yes?" The other was curious. "And that is—?"

"My wife."

"Your wife!" Taro stopped short. They were crossing the main street of Tokyo on foot.

"Yes," said the other, laughing boyishly, all his resentment against the girl lost and forgiven for the time being.

"And so you did it, after all?" said the other, with slow, bitter emphasis. His friend, then, was little different from other foreigners who marry only to desert.

"Did what?"

"Got a wife."

"Got a wife! Why, man, she came to me. She's a witch, the Sun-goddess herself. She's had me under her spell all these months. She has hypnotized me."

"And still has you under her spell?"

"I am wider awake to-day," said Jack, soberly.

"And soon," said Taro, "you will be still wider awake, and then—then it will be time for her to awaken."

"No!" said Jack, sharply, with bitter memory. "She has no heart whatever. She likes to pretend—that is all."

"How do you mean?"

"Simply that we've both been pretending and acting—I to myself, she to me; she trying to make me believe it was all real to her, at any rate these last two months; I trying to delude myself into believing in her, which was more than my conceit was good for, after all. Just when I was sure of her, I accidentally discovered that she was preparing to desert me altogether."

"She apparently has more sense than some of them," said Taro. "Her head rules her heart."

"Oh, entirely," Jack agreed, quickly, thinking of the money she had coaxed from him in the past.

"And you," Taro turned on him, "have you come out all right?"

"Perfectly!" the other laughed with a forced assurance and airiness that deceived Taro, who was somewhat credulous by nature. "It wasn't for a lifetime, you know," he added.

His reply was distasteful to the high moral sense of Taro Burton—more, it pained him, for it brought to him a sudden and deep disappointment in his friend. He changed the subject, and tried to talk about his own people. He was in a great hurry to go home, and would linger but a day in Tokyo. He had arrived sooner than they expected him. He was hungry for a sight of his little sister and mother—they were all he had in the world.

Jack's spirits were dampened for the moment, as he had expected his friend to remain with him for a few days. However, he got Taro's consent to accompany him to his home for dinner that evening, in order to meet the "Sun-goddess."

Taro was ushered with great ceremony into the quaint zashishi, which was supposed to be entirely Japanese, and was in reality wholly American, despite the screen, and mats and vases. Jack ran upstairs to prepare his wife to meet his friend.

The girl was panically dressing in her best clothes. The maid had brushed her hair till it glistened. Long ago her husband had peremptorily forbidden her the use of oil for the purpose of darkening or smoothing it, so it now shone a rich bronze black and curled entrancingly around her little ears and neck. She needed no color for her lips or cheeks; this also her husband had forbidden her to use. She looked like the picture of the Sun-goddess in some old fairy print, her eyes dancing and shining with excitement, her cheeks very red and rosy. She was irresistible, thought her husband, as he held her at arm's length. Then, to her great mortification and chagrin, he lifted her bodily in his arms and carried her downstairs. And thus they entered the room, the girl blushing and struggling in his arms.

Taro Burton was standing tall and erect, his back to the light. He was very grave, in spite of his friend's mirth, and, as Jack set the girl on the floor, he took a step forward to meet her, bowing ceremoniously in Japanese fashion.

Yuki stood up, straightened her crumpled gown, and hung her head a moment.

"Yuki, this is my friend, Mr. Burton."

She raised her head with a quick, terrified start, and then instantaneously hers and Taro's eyes met, and each recoiled and shrank backward, their eyes matching each other in the intense startled look of horror.

The man's face had taken on the color of death, and he was standing, immovable and silent, almost as if he were an image of stone. The girl sank to the floor in a confused heap, shivering and sobbing.

Jack turned from her to Taro, and then back again to the crouching girl. She was creeping on her knees towards Taro, but the man, having found the power of movement, went backward away from her, aged all in a moment.

He tried to turn his sick eyes from her, but they clung, fascinated as is the needle by the pole.

And then Jack's voice, hoarse with a fear he could not understand, broke in:

"Burton, what is the matter?"

Suddenly the girl sprang to her feet and rushed to Taro, sobbing and entreating in Japanese, but the terrible figure of the man remained immovable. Jack pulled her forcibly from him.

"Burton, dear old friend, what is it?"

The other pushed his hands from him with almost a blow.

"She is my sister! Oh, my God!"

Jack Bigelow felt for an instant as if the life within him had been stopped. Then he grasped at a chair and sank down dazed.

As though to break up the terrible silence, the girl commenced to laugh, but her laughter was terrible, almost unearthly. The man in the chair covered his face with his hands; the other made a movement towards her as if he would strike her. But she did not retreat: nay, she leaned towards him. And her laughter loud and discordant, sank low, and then faded in a tremulous sob.

She put out her little speaking, beseeching hands, and "Sayonara!" she whispered softly. Then there was stillness in the room, though the echoes seemed to repeat "Sayonara," "Sayonara," and again "Sayonara," and that means not merely "Farewell," but the heart's resignation: "If it must be."

Jack and Taro were alone together, neither breaking by a word the tragic sadness of that terrible silence. It was the coming into the room of the maid that recalled them to life. Twilight was settling. She brought the lighted andon and set it in the darkening room.

Jack got up slowly. The stupor and horror of it all were not gone from him, but he crossed to the other man, and looked into his dull, ashen face.

"My God! Burton, forgive me," he said, brokenly, "I am a gentleman. I will fix it all right. She is my wife, and all the world to me. We can re-marry if you wish, and I swear to protect her with all the love and homage I would give to any woman who became my wife."

"Yes, you must do that," said the other, with weak half-comprehension. "But where is she?"

"Where is she?" Jack repeated, dazedly. They had forgotten her departure. A dread of her possible loss possessed and stupefied Jack, and Taro was half-delirious.

"We must look for her at once," said Jack.

They called to her, and all over the house and through the grounds they searched for her, their lanterns scanning the dark shadows under the trees in the little garden; but only the autumn winds, sighing in the pine-trees, echoed her singing minor notes, and mocked and numbed their senses.

"She must have gone home," said the husband.

"We must go there at once," said the brother.

"It will be all right, Burton, dear old friend. Trust me; you know me well enough for that."

Taro paused, and turned on him burning eyes, in which friendliness had been replaced by a look that spoke of stern and awful judgment. "Otherwise," he began, but paused; then he went on in a cold hard voice, "I was going to say, I will kill you."

XIII.

In Which Two Men Learn of a Sister's Sacrifice

JACK Bigelow's usually sunny face was bleached to the ashiness of fear and despair. He was so nervous that he could not keep still a moment at a time, but would get up and pace the length of the car, only to return and look with eyes that attested the heartache within at the other man, silent and grim. Taro seemed the calmer, but well the younger man knew that beneath that subdued exterior slumbered a fire that needed but a breath to be turned into avenging fury.

At last they reached their destination. The little town once again! But this night Jack was not alone. There was no star or moon overhead to lighten their pathway; a dull, drizzly, sleety rain was falling. In silence they left the car; in silence plodded through the mud of the road and the damp grass of the field beyond. The little garden gate creaked on its hinges as they went through. They saw the dim outlines of the old palace before them, with its wide balconies and sloping roofs. Halfway up the garden was the family pond, freshened by a hidden spring, and the little winding brook which wound hither and thither showed how it emptied into the bay beyond. There was even a tiny boat moored on a toy-like island in the center of the pond.

For the first time Taro Burton paused, and looked with dreadful eyes at its dull surface, which even the darkness of the night and the miserable rain could not obliterate entirely. What were the memories that crowded back on him, suffocating him? Here it was that he and Yuki had grown up together. The little boat was the same, the island as small and neat, the house seemed as ever; nothing had changed. Yes, there was Yuki! A deep groan slipped from his lips.

There was a difference of seven years in their ages, but a stronger bond of sympathy and comradeship had existed between these two than is usual between brother and sister. Their nationality had to a large extent isolated them from other children, for the Japanese children had laughed at their hair and eyes, and called them "Kirishitans" (Christians). Until he was seven years of age, Taro had manfully, though bitterly, fought his battles alone. He had been a queer, brooding little lad, of passionate and violent temper, and, apparently, scorning any overtures of friendship from anyone outside his own household.

When the little sister had come, the boy had gone suddenly wild with joy, and had proceeded to bestow upon her the same worshipful love his mother gave exclusively to him, for Snowflake had been born when their English father lay at the gates of death, her tiny soul fluttering into life just as that of her father drifted outward into eternity, so that to Omatsu, the mother, who was passionately absorbed in her grief, her arrival had been a source of irritation. But Taro had carried her to the family temple, and had, himself, named her "Snowflake" (Yuki), for she had come at a time when all the land was covered with whiteness. There had been a frost and even a snowfall, which is rare in that part of the country. Moreover, she resembled a snowflake, so soft and white and pure.

How was it possible for him, after all these years, to come, as he now had come, once more to this place of which she had always been a part, and with which she had always been lovingly associated in his mind, and not be filled with emotions that rent his heart. She had been his inspiration and all the world to him.

He remembered how they would drift around in their tiny boat, and she, little autocrat, would perch before him, her eyes dancing and shining, while he told her the story of the fisherboy Urashima and his bride, the daughter of the dragon king. And when he would finish, for the hundredth time, perhaps, she would say, "See, Tarosama,[13] I am the princess, and you the fisherboy. We are sailing, sailing, sailing on the sea where Summer never dies," and he, to please her fancy, drifted on and on with her, around and around the little pond, until the sun began to sink in the west and the little mother would call them indoors.

Now the monotonous drip, drip, drip of the rain-drops as they plashed from the weeping willow-trees that surrounded the tiny lake fell upon its dull surface with mournful sound. Taro groaned again.

When he had knocked loudly a man came shuffling round from the rear of the house, and, in reply to his inquiry for Madam Omatsu, informed him gruffly that she had retired.

It did not matter; he must awaken her. Taro, who had found voice, told him with such insistence that the servant fled ignominiously to obey him. They waited for some time, out in the melancholy night. There was no sound from within the house. Taro hammered on the door once more.

---

[13] *Sama* is a form of respectful or affectionate address in Japanese. It is attached to the person's first or last name, as it is here: "Taro-sama."

Then a faint light appeared from a window close by the door, and the man's head showed again. He begged their honorable patience. He would open [it] in a fraction of a second. He was very humble and servile now, and, as he admitted them, backed before them, bowing and bobbing at every step, for his mistress's entire household had been taught to treat foreigners with the greatest deference and respect.

"Go to your mistress," said Taro, briefly, "and tell her that her son desires to see her at once."

There was immediately a fluttering at the other side of the shoji. Taro saw an eye withdraw from a hole. There were a few minutes of silence, and then the shoji parted and a woman entered the room. Her mother-love must have prompted her to rush into the arms of her son, for she had not seen him in five years, but, whatever her emotions, she skillfully concealed them, for the paltry reason that her son was accompanied by a stranger, an honorable foreign friend, and it behooved her to affect the finest manners. Consequently she prostrated herself gracefully, bowing and bowing, until Taro strode rapidly over to her and lifted her to her feet.

She was quite pretty and very gentle and graceful. Her face, oval in contour, was smooth and unwrinkled as a girl's, for Japanese women age slowly. It was hard to believe she was the mother of the tall man now holding her at arm's length and looking down at her with such deep, questioning eyes.

"Where is my sister, Yuki?" he demanded, hoarsely.

"Yuki?" Madam Omatsu smiled with saintly confidence. She had retired. Would they pray wait till morning? Ah, how was her honorable son, her august offspring? She began fondling her boy now, stroking his face, standing on tiptoe to kiss it, ecstatically smoothing and caressing his hands, feeling his strange clothes, and laughing joyously at their likeness to those of her dead husband's. But the dark shadow on Taro's face was deepening, nor would he return or submit to his mother's caresses till his fears regarding his sister were stilled.

"Send for her," he said, briefly, and she knew he would not be gainsaid.

Send for her! Ah, Madam Omatsu begged her noble son's pardon ten million times, but she had made a great mistake. His sister had, of course, retired, but it was not within their augustly miserable and honorably unworthy domicile. She had gone out on a visit to some friends.

Taro undid the clinging hands and pushed her from him, his brooding eyes glaring.

"Where?"

Where? Why, it was only a short distance—perhaps two rice-fields' lengths from their house.

"The house?—the people's name?"

Madam Omatsu whitened a trifle. Her eyes narrowed, her lips quivered. She tried once more frantically to prevaricate.

The people's name? She could not quite recall, but the next day—the next day surely—

"Ah-h," said her son, with delirious brutality, "you are deceiving me, lying to me. I demand to know where she is. I am her rightful guardian. I must see her at once."

Madam Omatsu protested with faint vehemence, but she did not weep. She even essayed a little laugh, that reminded Jack eerily of Yuki. In the dimly lighted room she looked strangely like her daughter, save that she was much smaller and quite thin and frail whereas Yuki was rosy and healthy.

Taro was speaking to her in Japanese, in a sharp, cruel voice, and she was answering gently, meekly, humbly, consolingly. Jack felt sorry for her. Suddenly Taro threw her hands from him with a gesture of sheer despair and exhausted patience.

"I can learn nothing from her, nothing," he said in English. Then he turned on her again. "Listen," he said. "You are my mother, and as such I honor you, but you must not deceive me. I know all; know that my sister was married to an American; know how she was married, if you call such marriage. They do not consider it so, as you must know. What do you know of this, my mother? It could not have happened without your knowledge?"

The mother broke down at last. All was indeed lost if he knew that much. She sank in a heap at his feet, and again the other man was reminded of her daughter.

Taro raised her, not ungently, curbing his emotions.

"Pray speak to me the truth," he implored.

"It was for you," she said, faintly, in Japanese. "I desired it, I, your mother; and, afterwards, she also, she, your sister. It was a small sacrifice, my son."

"Sacrifice! What do you mean?" he cried.

"Alas, we had not the money to keep you at the American school. And later, when you desired to return, it was still harder."

"Oh, my God!"

She went on, speaking brokenly in Japanese. After he had gone to America their little fortune had been swept away, but of this they had kept him in ignorance, fearing that he would not remain in the university did he know how poor they had become. The house belonged to him; they could not sell it. There had been but poor crops in their few remaining acres of rice-fields; their income became smaller and smaller. One by one their servants and coolies[14] had to be sacrificed, till there were only a very few left, and these refused to be paid for their services. They had secured money in what manner they could, and sent it to him. It was hard, but they loved him.

Then Yuki, unknown to her mother, had gone up to Tokyo each day and learned the arts of the geisha; later she invented dances and songs of her own, and soon she was able to command a good price at one of the chief tea-gardens in Tokyo.

This for a season had brought them in a fair income, and for a time they were enabled to send him even more than the usual allowance. Then came his request for his passage money. Alas! they were but weak and silly women. They had forgotten to save against this event in their desire to keep him in comfort. Nakodas had approached Yuki, and tempting offers were made to her. She had resisted all of them, for she was then below the age when girls usually marry, but sixteen years of age. Only when it became imperative to raise the passage money would she even listen to the persuasion of her mother and of the nakoda. They had pointed out to her the great advantage, and finally, as the brother's letters grew more insistent, she had broken down and given in. After that time she had assisted them in their efforts to secure her a suitable husband. They had been exceptionally successful, for she had married a foreigner who would likely leave her soon, which was fortunate in Omatsu's mind, one whose excellent virtues and whose wealth were above question. This was all there was to tell. She prayed and besought her honorable son's pardon.

During her recital Taro had leaned towards her, listening with bated breath to every word that escaped her lips. His thin, nervous face was horribly drawn, his hands were clenched tightly at his side, his whole form was quivering. He tried to regain his scattered senses, and his hand vaguely wandered to his brow, pushing back the thick black hair that had fallen over it.

"You cannot understand," he said to the other man, his voice scarcely recognizable for its labor. "It was for me, me, my little sister sold herself. To keep me in comfort and ease! Snowflake for me! And they kept me in ignorance. I did not even dream they were in straitened circumstances.

---

[14] Eaton's reference to coolies (a derogatory term for Chinese laborers) indicates her somewhat superficial knowledge of Japanese culture—a deficiency that escaped the notice of most of her readership.

Oh, had I not willing hands and an eager heart to work, to slave for them? Why should the whole burden have fallen on her, my little, frail sister? But it has always been so. There is no such thing as justice in this land for the woman."

Jack heard him raving, understood, and bowed his head in impotent sorrow.

"Has your mother given you any information of her whereabouts?" he suddenly broke in.

Taro had forgotten that they were seeking her. His mother's story had held all his attention. The horror aroused by that recital of devotion, the thought of the months of her sweet life which she had sacrificed for him, and then how he had repulsed her, addressed on his poor, numbed senses. But Jack's inquiry recalled him. A thousand dark surmises regarding her overwhelmed him.

"Yes, yes—where is she?" he asked, huskily.

She had been with her husband some days now. Madam Omatsu expected her home soon, and this time she would never again return to him.

Taro's eyes were inflamed. "And she has not returned? She should be here now! Ah, it is plain to be seen what has happened. She may be taking her life at this moment. It is what a Japanese girl would do. She has the blood of heroes in her veins; she would not falter."

All of a sudden he turned upon his friend. Then the full agony caused by his sister's disappearance and her great sacrifice descended upon him, and he tottered. Before Jack could stay him, he swayed forward and, as he fell, struck his forehead upon the comer of a heavy chair that had been his father's. When Jack raised the head of the unconscious man he found blood flowing from a wide cut over the left eye.

There were hurrying feet throughout the house, terrified whispers, and sobs, and above all, a mother's voice raised in terrible anguish.

XIV.

A Struggle in the Night

By day and night they kept their unrelaxing watch by the bedside of the sick man. Ever he tossed and turned and muttered and cried aloud, one word alone on his lips—his sister's name.

Tenderly the mother smoothed the fevered brow, softly she stroked the restless hands, and tried to still their fever between her own cool, soothing ones. Thin lines had traced their shadows on her worn face; gray threads had come to mingle with the glossy black of her hair. But she never permitted herself, after that first night of anguish, to betray her emotions, for, if she did, well she knew she would be refused the precious labor of nursing her boy. And she kept her sleepless, tireless watch night and day. Her maid begged her to lie down herself and rest, but she shook her head with bright, dry eyes. Rest for her? While he lay tossing thus? Nay! perhaps when he should find the rest, the gods would permit her also a respite; till then she must keep her watch.

She smiled pathetically when the white-faced American boy tried to insist that she should sleep, with the little air of authority he had assumed in the household. But with the gentle smile she also shook her head in negation.

"Let me take your place," he pleaded. "He is dear to me also."

Still she smiled, such a shadowy, heart-aching smile, and turned back to the sick-bed.

Jack Bigelow went back to Tokyo, and began his vigilant search for the missing girl. The services of the entire metropolitan police board were called forth, and money was not spared.

The nakoda who had brought about their marriage was put through a vigorous catechism, but he could tell them nothing. The proprietor of the tea-garden swore she had not returned to him, and when he bewailed the misfortune which was filling his house and gardens with officers, Jack consoled him by paying liberally for the loss he claimed he was suffering.

On the fifth day the mystery of the girl's disappearance still remained unsolved. Large rewards were offered for a clue to her whereabouts. The police were sure that she was somewhere in Tokyo, and Jack urged them to continue their unremitting search in the city, but each night dawned upon their fruitless efforts. Now someone had seen a girl of her description entering a tea-house on the eve of her disappearance; another had seen her selling flowers in the market-place; and yet another swore she had gone on board a German vessel with a dried-up foreigner. This last person could not be mistaken—a Japanese girl with blue eyes and red hair. But each clue was found wanting and proved false.

Then back to Yuki's home, sick-hearted, disappointed, weary, went Jack Bigelow. A servant met him with the blessed news that the man down with brain fever was improving; that a merciful calm had at last come to him, and that now he slept. Wearied from his fruitless endeavors to find some clue to Yuki's whereabouts, the first good news in days unnerved the young man. He sat down, covering his eyes with his hands. He was badly in need of rest himself, but his mind was full of the mother in the sick-room overhead.

Madam Omatsu, was she resting?

No, she still kept her watch, but she was very weak, and they feared she would break down if they could not prevail on her to rest.

Jack went slowly up the stairs, tapped softly on the shoji, and then entered the sick-room.

Taro lay on the heavy English bed, with its white coverlets and curtains, his face upturned.

"You must rest," Jack whispered to the woman with the wan face and wasted form, kneeling by the bedside.

She shook her head, resisting.

"I beg you to," pleaded Jack, and, though she could not understand him, she knew what he was saying, and still resisted.

"Come," he said, gently, and put his hands upon her shoulders. "See, he sleeps now. It is well, and you will be too weak and faint to minister to him when he awakes, otherwise."

But she protested that her health was excellent; that she would not leave her son. He stooped down, and attempted to raise her gently to her feet, but she would not permit him.

He saw the tired droop of the eyes. "She will fall asleep soon," he said to himself, and so sat down beside her, putting his arm about her and pillowing her head on his shoulder. She did not restrain him. She looked gratefully into the frank, inviting eyes. She sighed, her head wavered and dropped. The room was very still and silent. Gradually the woman fell asleep, and as she slept she sighed from ineffable weariness.

Jack looked towards the silent figure on the bed. The grayness of the approaching night gave the face an expression that was sinister in the extreme. He shuddered and averted his face. The little form in his arms grew heavier.

"She will rest better lying down," he thought, and carried her into the adjoining room and laid her softly down. Then he took the lighted andon, and, carrying it into the sick-room, set it in a comer near the bed, and drew down the shutters. After this, he went back to the bed, and stood for a minute looking down on the sleeping man, an expression of infinite sadness on his face. Taro stirred, the hand lying outside the coverlet contracted, then closed spasmodically; the expression of the face became terrifying. He moaned. It seemed to Jack as if the sleeping man was haunted by a terrible nightmare which robbed him of the rest that should have found him.

And it was with Taro as Jack had thought. He was in the midst of a fever dream—a nightmare. He thought his little sister, Snowflake, knelt by his bedside and soothed and ministered to his wants. He felt rested and at peace at last; but, alas! just as he was slipping into happy oblivion, a dark form loomed up beside his sister, bent over, and clutched at her. She struggled wildly at first, then weakly; finally her struggles ceased, and she lay very still and white. The man lifted her up and carried her away. After a time he came back, and now Taro felt his breath on his own face. He was bending over him. In a dim haze he saw the face, and recognized it as that of his friend, Jack Bigelow! He tried to reach out and grasp him, to strike and kill him, but he was at the mercy of some invisible power which benumbed him and held him down. His limbs refused to move, he was unable to lift so much as a finger, stir an eyelash, and all the time the man's breath was on his face, stealing into his nostrils and suffocating him.

Jack noted the gasping of his friend with alarm, and stooped over for the purpose of removing the pillow to give him relief. But at the touch of his hand, as he attempted to raise the head on the pillow, the life blood started vividly, madly, through the man on the bed, and suddenly he had sprung into wild life. Jack saw the terrible gleam of two delirious eyes, and stood magnetized. With lightning fury the raving man had thrown aside the bedclothes, sprung from the bed, and thrown himself on the other with such force that the two came to the ground together, the madman on top.

"I have you now!—traitor! betrayer!" he said, as his hands felt Jack's warm throat.

Jack had been taken so by surprise that he was dazed in the first moment, and in the next realized that he was powerless to defend himself. He was in the grasp of one temporarily insane, one whose lithe, physical strength he already knew well. It would be useless to fight against that strength. His salvation lay in being passive and feigning unconsciousness; but could he do this with those terrible fingers closing around his throat, throttling the life out of him? Now they pressed hard, now relaxed, now caressed his neck and throat, rubbed it, pinched only to press again. He was playing with him! Jack did not stir. He had closed his eyes, and was praying for strength to meet unflinchingly whatever fate held for him.

"Where have you put her?" came the fierce whisper, close to his ear. "Where did you carry her to? Hah! you are silent. Have I silenced you like this and this? You are cold; you cannot breathe now, nor smile nor laugh at her. No, not while I have my hand here to press so, and so. Once you were my friend, and I loved you. But now—so you killed her! Now I will kill you like this, and this, and this!"

Jack was becoming weaker and weaker. The white-shrouded figure sitting on him leaned forward, staring dreadfully, but his victim saw nothing, heard nothing. Suddenly it seemed as if another had sprung upon him and was beating his life out. He dimly heard a woman's cries, and, intermingled, a terrible laughter. Then life and consciousness seemed to depart, and he knew no more.

When he regained consciousness he found himself on a bed. A woman was leaning over him, bathing his head, smoothing and caressing it—a woman with an angelic face, so like Yuki's when she had nursed him during a brief illness that in his weakness he fainted at the mere dream of her sweet presence. But it was not Yuki; it was the mother. She had been awakened by the talking and cries in the sick-room, and, rushing to the door, had looked in on the terrible scene.

Japanese women have little or no fear of physical disaster for themselves. She raised a fearful cry to arouse the household, then flung herself on the two men, and with her puny strength sought to divide them. At first her son laughed and resisted her, but when her white face flashed before him his grip grew weak, and he staggered back, dazed by the rush of returning reason. He, too, had taken her for the ghost of his lost sister!

The alarmed household had flocked into the room. Gently they prevailed on him to return once more to the bed, as weak as a child now.

Jack was not seriously hurt. In his shattered, nervous condition, however, the shock had temporarily unhinged him, and for several days he lay in bed, waited on and attended by the gentle Omatsu, who went like a sweet, soothing spirit back and forth between the two rooms, who called him "son," and was to him as if she were indeed his mother, till she could not approach him but he kissed her hands and blessed her from his heart.

XV.
The Vow

THE happy sadness of the brown autumn had faded in a yellow gleam of light. December had entered the land with a little drift of frost and snow which had surprised the country, for December is not usually a cold month in Japan. Its advent shook the little housewives into action and life. New mats of rice straw were being laid, and every nook and corner dusted with fresh, bamboo brooms and dusters, for the Japanese begin to prepare a month in advance for the New Year season, and all the country seems to wake into active life and present a holiday appearance.

But the old palace, where dwelt the Burton family, kept its garment of perpetual gloom, and stood out in mocking contrast to the neighboring houses. No window was thrown open, no door turned in to air the place and give it the sunshine of the coming New Year.

Thick as the dust that had gathered about its unkept rooms, the shadow of death pervaded the place. Vast shadows, mysterious and oppressive, crept in, enshrouding it with their ghostly presence. From afar off the drone of a curfew bell was heard, its slow, mournful cadence seeming to drift into a dirge. Outside the early winds of winter were wailing a requiem, and all the spirits of the air floated about and beat against the sombre palace.

At dusk consciousness returned to the dying man, and weakly, though intelligently, he looked about him, and even smiled faintly at the wailing and moaning that crept upward from the rooms below, where the few old retainers of the household, who had been in the service of the family long before Taro had been born, and had stayed by them after their fortunes had fallen, were huddled together and loudly lamenting the approaching death of the son of the house.

Before a tiny shrine in a corner of the room was the prostrate form of the mother. Her lips were dumb, but her speaking eyes wailed out her prayer to all the gods for mercy. And at the bedside, his face in his hands, knelt Jack Bigelow. Perhaps he, too, was praying to the one and only God of his people.

"Burton," he said, as the sick man stirred, "you have something to say to me?"

He bent over and wiped the dews that lay thick as a frost on lips and brow.

"My sister—" Taro began with painful slowness.

"My wife—" whispered the other, his voice breaking, and then, as Taro seemed unable to proceed, he put his mouth close down to his ear.

"Burton, our grief is a common one. I swear by everything I hold sacred and holy that I will never cease in my efforts to find my wife! Nothing that strength or money can do shall be spared. I will take no rest till she is found. Before God, I will right this wrong I have unconsciously done you and yours and mine!"

Taro's eyes, wide and bright, fixed Jack's steadfastly. His long, thin hand stirred and quivered, and attempted to raise itself. Without a word Jack took it in his own. He had understood that mute effort to mean belief and confidence in him. And, kneeling there in the melancholy dusk, he held Taro's hand between his own until it was stiff and cold.

Whither had the soul of the Eurasian drifted? Out and along the interminable and winding journey to the Meido of his maternal ancestors, or to give an account of itself to the great Man-God-three-in-one-Creator of his father?

The mother crept from the shrine with stealing step, her white face like a mask of death, her small, frail hands outstretched, like those of one gone blind.

A consciousness of her eerie approach thrilled Jack Bigelow. He dropped Taro's hand and turned towards her, standing before and hiding the sight of the dead from her. In the dim shadows of the deepening twilight she looked as frail and ethereal as a wraith, for she had clothed herself in all the vestal garments of the dead.

With somewhat of the heroism of her feudal ancestors Omatsu had prepared herself to face and undertake that perilous journey to the unknown with her son. In the pitiful tangled reasoning that had wrestled in the bosom of this Japanese woman, always there had disturbed the beauty of such a sacrifice the doubt as to whether the gods would indeed receive her with this son of hers who had dedicated his soul to an alien and strange God. But she had prepared herself to risk the consequences. And now she stood there swaying and tottering in all her ghastly attire, while opposite to her stood the tall, fair-haired foreigner with the pitying gray eyes of her own dead lord.

She essayed to speak, but her voice was barely above a parched whisper.

"Anata?" (Thou). It was a gentle word, spoken as a question, as though she would ask him, "Condescend to speak your honorable desire with me?"

"Mother!" he only said—"dear mother!"

At Taro's funeral Jack Bigelow made the acquaintance of his wife's family. He had not imagined it possible for anyone to have so many relatives. They came from all parts of the country, distant and close cousins and uncles and aunts, and even an old grandfather and grandmother, the former very decrepit and quite blind. And they all lined up in order, and wept real or artificial tears and muttered prayers for the soul of the dead boy.

A few of them were rich and important men of high rank in Japan; some of them were suave and courteous, coming merely for form's sake and for the honor of the family; most of them were of the type of the decayed gentility of Japan—poor but proud, dignified but humble in their dignity.

They all regarded Jack with the same grave, stoical gaze peculiar to the better-class Japanese, betraying in no way by their expression surprise or resentment at his presence among them. As a matter of fact, none of the family were aware of the relation in which he stood to them, and so had occasion for no real animus against him, regarding him merely as a friend of Taro's. But in his supersensitive condition Jack imagined that they looked upon him as an intruder, perhaps as one who had brought distress and havoc upon their household.

When, however, after the funeral the little mob of friends and relatives had gradually dispersed till there was none left besides himself and Omatsu, the intense loneliness and silence of the big house grated upon his nerves, so that he would have welcomed the wailing of the servants, which had now been buried in the grave.

Omatsu, too, who had borne herself with heroic fortitude and bravery all through the day, now that the reaction had come, was shivering and trembling, and, when he approached her with a pitying exclamation, she went to him straightway and cried in his arms like a little, tired child. He comforted her with broken words, though his own tears were falling on her little, bowed head. And he tried to tell her, in terribly bad pidgin Japanese—something Yuki had taught him—how it would be his care to protect and guard her in the future just as if she were indeed his mother; that he was not worthy, but he would try to fill the place of the beautiful boy who was sleeping his last sleep. And he told of the promise he had given to Taro, how his life would be devoted to but one end and purpose, to find his wife. Would she accompany him?

She entreated him to take her with him. But in the end, after all, she could not accompany him. Her health, which had never been robust, gave way to her grief, and Jack took her back to her parents, for it was necessary that he should spare no time from his search, and, moreover, she was too delicate to travel. Before leaving her he saw to it that she and her parents should have every comfort possible.

The old palace, grim, gray, and haggard in the winter landscape, was now completely deserted. The townspeople looked askance at it, as at a haunted house, knowing somewhat of the tragedy that hid within its closed portals.

Jack was the last to leave the place. Omatsu had begged him to see to the closing up, and the paying off of all the old servants. When he had finally come out he was shocked at the curious crowd of neighbors who had gathered about the gates and were whispering and gossiping about him and waiting for him. But they were quite respectful and silent as he passed them. He was an object of curiosity, this tall foreigner who had married among them, and they watched him with round, wondering eyes, following him all the way to the station, a little, pygmy procession, very much as children follow a circus. Once or twice he half turned as though to tell them to leave him, but stopped himself in time, remembering how strange he must really seem to them.

At the station he bowed to them gravely, and his bow was solemnly and politely returned by those in front. And it was in this strangely pathetic though grotesque manner that the tall, fair-haired barbarian left the town.

Less than a year before he had been a lighthearted, joyous boy. He was now a man, with a burden on his soul and a sacred task to perform, there was an awful abyss in his life that must be bridged. Never again would life have for him the same rosy bow of promise, not until he had found that other part of his soul—his Sun-goddess.

XVI.

A Pilgrim of Love

JACK Bigelow went up to Yokohama, where the Tokyo detectives thought they had a clue to the girl's whereabouts. A new and very beautiful geisha had appeared among the dancing-girls, and as no one seemed to know anything about her history it was thought that she might be the missing Yuki. But she had disappeared only the day before his arrival there.

Jack spent a month in the big metropolis, shadowing the tea-gardens, and watching, with the assistance of men he had hired, every geisha house and garden; but though many girls apparently answering to the description of Yuki were brought before him, none of them proved to be the missing girl, and the disgust the young man experienced at their total unlikeness to his wife was only equaled by his bitter disappointment.

A telegram from police headquarters brought him back to Tokyo. Here he was told that the detectives had traced the missing girl to Nagasaki, a seaport on the western coast of Kyushu. This was the city where Yuki's father had first lived in Japan. He had been the son of a rich silk merchant, and had come to Japan in order to extend his knowledge of the silk trade and expand his father's business. But Stephen Burton had become infatuated with the country, had married a Japanese wife, assimilated the ways of her people, and in time had even become a naturalized citizen. He never returned alive to his native England, though strange, cold, red-bearded men had taken his body from the wife, and had crossed the seas with it.

Old Sir Stephen Burton had never forgiven what he considered the *mésalliance* of his son, and hence Taro and Yuki had never seen or known any of their father's people, and he himself had died while they were yet children.

Some feeling of sentiment might have brought Yuki to this place. Moreover, there were many public tea-houses there, where she could quickly find employment. The police were positive in their statements that they were not mistaken in the identity of the girl they claimed to be Yuki.

Traveling by slow and tedious trains, with no sleeping accommodations and but few of the modem luxuries that are necessities on American trains; traveling by kurumma, with the flying heels of his runners scattering the dust of the highway in his eyes, when the landscape before, behind, and around him seemed a maze of dazzling blue; traveling on foot, when he was too restless to do otherwise than tramp, he was weary and ill when he finally reached Nagasaki. Here an amazing horde of nakodas pestered him with their offerings of matrimonial happiness. He had no heart for them. They stifled him with memories that were better left sleeping.

The tea-house to which he had been directed was owned and run by an elderly geisha, who, in her day, had been noted for her own beauty and cleverness. She was all affectation and grace now. She met Jack with exaggerated expressions of welcome, and in a sweet, sibilant voice pressed upon him the comforts and entertainments of her "poor place."

He did not pause to exchange compliments with her.

Was there not in her house a girl, very beautiful and very young, who sang and danced?

Madam Pine-leaf (that was her name) allowed her face to betray surprised amusement at the question. Why, her place was famous for the beauty of her maidens, and every one of them danced and sang more bewitchingly than the fairies themselves. But she only said, very humbly: "My maidens are all unworthily fair, and all of them indulge in the honorable dance and song. It is part of the accomplishment of every geisha."

"Yes, but you could not mistake this girl. She is distinct from all others. She—her eyes are blue. She is only half Japanese!"

"Ah-h!—a half-caste." Madam Pine-leaf's lips formed in a *moue*. She was very polite, however. She pretended to consult her mind. Then she begged that he would remain, at all events, and see for himself all her girls.

Impatiently he waited, a terrible nervousness taking possession of him at the mere possibility that Yuki might be near him. But though he scanned with almost seeming rudeness the faces of the inmates of the place, none of them was like unto her whom he sought. When he paid his hostess, who, recognizing in him a generous patron, had been careful to stay close by him the entire evening, his face betrayed his exceeding disappointment.

The woman glanced at the big fee in her hand, and a feeling of pity and gratitude called up all her native prevarication.

Now that she had spent the whole evening turning the matter over in her mind, she recalled the fact that only a few days before a girl answering exactly to his description of his wife had worked for her for a short period, but unfortunately she had left her and gone to Osaka.

Madam Pine-leaf's face was guileless, her words convincing. There was gentle compassion in her eyes, which added to the comfort of her words.

Jack wrung her slim hands gratefully till they ached.

Osaka? How far away was that? Did Madam Pine-leaf believe he had time to get there before she would leave? What was the exact address?

Yes, she believed he would be in time, and she drew out a dainty tablet and wrote an address upon it, and with deep and graceful obeisances she prayed that the gods would accompany and guide him.

He reached Osaka at night, when its many strange canals and narrow rivers were reflecting the lights of the city, like glittering spear-heads, on their dark, shining surface. The hotel was miles from the station, but the streets were deserted, and there was no traffic to hinder the flying feet of his runner. At night the city seemed strangely romantic and peaceful, a spot that would have attracted one of Yuki's temperament. But daylight revealed it as it was—a bustling commercial center, where everybody seemed hurrying as though bent on accomplishing some important mission.

Jack stayed but a few days in Osaka. She was not there. The proprietor of the Osaka gardens, hearing his story, humbly apologized for the fact that while such a girl had honored for a short season his unworthy gardens, she had left him now some days ago. Whither had she gone? To Kyoto.

And in Kyoto, the most fascinating and beautiful city in all Japan, he was sent from one tea-house to another, each proprietor acknowledging that one answering to the description had been in his employ, but declaring that she had left only a short time previous. She was only a visiting geisha, who moved from place to place.

Finally he traced her back to Tokyo, the place whence he had started on his weary pilgrimage. She was the chief geisha, so he was told, of the Sanzaeyenion gardens. With his brain swimming, his lips almost refusing him speech, he went straightway to this place. The proprietor received him with magnificent humility, and, listening to his disjointed questions, answered that all was well. She was even then within his honorably miserable tea-house. For the privilege of seeing her he would be obliged to make an honorably insignificant charge, and, if he (the august barbarian) desired to take her away with him, a further fee must be forthcoming.

Waiving these questions aside, by putting down so much coin that the little proprietor's eyes matched its glisten, he followed him up the stairway to the private quarters of the more important geishas. Into one of the rooms he was unceremoniously ushered.

A girl who sat on a mat put forward her two hands, and her bowed head on top of them. Jack watched her with bated breath. He could not see her face, and the room was badly lighted. But when he could bear no longer her perpetual bowing and had lifted her, with hands that shook, to her feet, he saw her face. It was that of a stranger!

A slight illness now hindered the progress of his search, but he would not allow himself the rest he needed; and still ill, haggard, and a shadow of his former self, the young man once more drifted to the metropolitan police station.

They had exhausted all their clues, but they were kind-hearted little men, these Japanese policemen. The chief of police invented a story that would have done credit to one of Japan's poets.

Yuki was somewhere in the vicinity of Matsushima Bay,[15] on the north-eastern coast of Japan, near the city of Sendai, where the waters flow into the Pacific. This was a spot favored by unhappy lovers, and the chief of police had positive evidence that a girl answering to her description had been seen wandering daily in that part of the country. He even produced a telegraph blank, with an indecipherable message in Japanese characters written on it, purporting to give this information. His advice to the young man was to go to this honorable place and stay there for some time. The country was large thereabouts. He might not find her at once, but soon or late surely she would turn up there.

Jack was impressed with his glib recital, and then, moreover, he remembered that Yuki had told him much about this place, which they had planned to visit together some day. He started straightway for it, buoyed up with a hope he had not known in months.

And the chief of police snapped his fingers and bobbed his head and clinked the big fee he had received.

"These foreign devils are naive," he said to an assistant.

The cringing assistant agreed. "They believe any august lie," he replied.

His superior frowned. "It was for his good, after all," he returned, tartly.

In the city of Sendai Jack put up at a small Japanese hostelry, and from there each day he would start out and wander down to the beach of the wonderful bay. It was all as Yuki had pictured it, with her vivid, passionate imagery. There were the countless rocks of all sizes and forms scattered in it, with strange, shapely pine-trees growing up from them, and the one

---

[15] Matsushima Bay is a legendary site for the suicide of star-crossed lovers, particularly young women, who drown themselves in despair after losing a lover.

bare rock called "Hadakajima," or "Naked Island," and all the beautiful romances, impossible and dreamy as the fairy tales of a classic Oriental poet, that she had woven about and around this place, came back to his mind now, haunting him like a beautiful dream, until the memory of her, and the influence of the beauty of the place, seemed to cast a mystic spell all about him.

For, oh! the scenes that enwrapped the bay! The slopes and hillocks and the great mountains beyond were garbed in vestal white, pure and glistening. The snowflakes had tipped the branches of the pine, and there they hung, like glistening pearl-drops, sometimes dropping with little bounds on the rocks, there to freeze or melt into the bay.

And some vague fancy, baffling in its hopelessness, nevertheless, clung to him that possibly she might have come hither to this peaceful spot, far from the scenes where they had loved and suffered so deeply, for, with unerring insight, Jack knew that she had loved him. Bit by bit he traced backward in his mind every proof she had given him of this, and now, when the sorrow of her loss seemed more than he could bear, the knowledge of this upheld and cheered him always. But the beauty of Matsushima could give him no peace of mind or soul, for he was alone! The stillness and silence of the very atmosphere, the tall pine-trees, bending gracefully in the swaying, swinging breezes, seemed to mock him with their calm content. The bay was enchanted—yes, but haunted too—haunted by the imagination of the little feet that had perhaps wandered along its shore.

In a little village only a short distance from the beach, inhabited by a few simple, honest fisher-folk, Jack tried to ascertain whether they had seen aught of her he sought. But they babbled fairy stories back at him. There had been many, many witchmaids who had haunted the shores of Matsushima; many young girls, who had lost their minds through unfortunate love affairs, had wandered thither. They were the ghosts of these unfortunate lovers, who had sought in death the bliss of love denied them in life, which now haunted the shore of the bay.

That the strange, fair man who had lost his bride would meet the same untimely though poetic fate the simple people never doubted.

And so, like one who has lost his soul, he wandered hither and thither throughout the islands of Japan in search of it.

Sunshine had been the dominant element in Jack Bigelow's character, and in a less degree impulsiveness and generosity. No one had ever given him credit for intensity of feeling or greatness of purpose. But sometimes tribulation will bring out such qualities, which have lain hidden beneath an apparently superficial exterior.

A deep, abiding love for his summer bride had sprung into eternal life in his heart. She was never absent from his mind. There were moments when for a time he would forget his immeasurable loss, and would drift into memory, and in fancy re-live with her that dream summer. She had become the soul of him. She would remain in his heart until it ceased to beat.

XVII.

Yuki's Wanderings

HAD Jack followed Yuki on the night she went out of his house and life, he would have known that she was not to be found in all Japan. She had hurried from his and Taro's presence with but one object—to take herself forever from the sight of the brother whom she had loved but who had repulsed her, whom she had dishonored in trying to assist. She took the road for Tokyo, and, head downward, sobbing like a little child who has lost its way in the dark, stumbled blindly along until she had come within its limits.

She had no idea whither she was going now, what she would do; her mind could only contain her grief. But as she wandered aimlessly about, weeping silently, an address slipped itself into her consciousness—the address written on the card handed her by the American theatrical man months before, when he had followed her from the tea-house. She had studied the card curiously at the time, and now, though the name had escaped her—she had really never been able to make it out—her mind still held the address.

She turned in the direction in which she knew the American's house lay, and at length found it, wearied both by the anguish of her mind and by her long walk. Yes, the American gentleman was in, said the garrulous Japanese servant who answered her timid summons. He had returned from lands far south less than a week ago, and now in two more days he would be off again. Did she want to meet him? Perhaps he slept.

Yuki said she would speak with him but a minute, and the servant vanished. Almost immediately the manager appeared before her, frowning heavily. But at sight of her his face brightened wonderfully.

"Why, if it ain't the girl I heard sing at the tea-garden!" he cried. "Come right inside."

And he eagerly drew her, unresisting, within.

Two days later, on board the *Yokohama Maru*, Yuki left her native Japan.

As the ship weighed anchor, she closed her eyes and faintly clung to the guard-rail. All about her she could hear the passengers talking and laughing, a few were cheering and waving flags and handkerchiefs to friends on shore. And long after the wharf was only a dim, shadowy outline she still clung there to the rail, her hands cold and tense.

Someone put an arm about her, and she started as though she had been struck.

"You are not ill already, you poor little thing?" said a woman's clear, pleasing voice.

Yuki regarded her piteously. She dimly recognized in her the wife of her employer, and she struggled to regain her scattered wits, but vainly. She was only able to look up into the sympathetic face of the other with eyes which could not conceal the turbulent tragedy of her soul.

"Why, you are shivering all over, and are as cold as—Jimmy, come over here," she turned and called peremptorily to her husband, who hastened forward, throwing his cigar overboard.

"Look here; she's sick already. Better send one of those ayah women, or whatever you call 'em, over, and have her put to bed right away."

They undressed her, submissive as a little child, and put her into the berth of a little stateroom, which seemed to Yuki, who had never in her life before been on board a vessel of any sort, save the tiny craft about the rivers at her home, like a tiny cage or vault, wherein she, exhausted and weary, had been put to die.

She lay there with the surging bustle of the ship's noises overhead and the tremulous growl of the waters beneath the ship droning in her ears like the melancholy ringing of a dying curfew-bell at twilight.

The ayah reported to the manager's wife, an ex-comic-opera prima donna, that she was resting and sleeping; but when that impetuous, big-hearted woman peeped in on her, she found Yuki's eyes wide open. She whirled into the small stateroom, almost filling it with her large person, and sat down beside the poor little weary girl and looked at her with friendly and approving eyes.

"You are like a pretty picture on a fan," she said; "the prettiest Japanese girl I've seen. I think we'll be fine friends, don't you?"

Yuki could only assent with a weary little nod of her head. She closed her eyes.

"You are not so dreadfully sick, are you?" said the American. "I thought maybe we could have a nice little gossip together. You see, my husband's the boss of this whole outfit that we've got along with us, and I don't know that there's one of the whole lot I've ever cared to associate with before. You're different. Now, ain't I good to speak out just what's on my mind, eh?"

"I ought to *thang* you," said Yuki, feebly, "but I am too weary to be perlite."

"Then you shall be left alone, you child, you," said the other; then she kissed Yuki lightly, and went out of the door.

But after she had gone Yuki's passivity left her. She sat up quivering, and then with nervous quickness she began to dress herself. She could not open the door of the stateroom. She was unused to strange doors that required the pushing of springs and bolts. She had lived in a land where bolts and locks were almost unknown, where a shoji fell apart at a touch of a hand.

Now she pushed hard against the door, but, as she had not turned the handle, it refused to move. A terror possessed her that they had locked her in this tiny, awful cell, to which penetrated no light save that which filtered through a small porthole against which the waters beat and beat.

She flung herself desperately against the door, battering it with her tiny hands; she felt herself growing dizzy and blind as the ship rocked and swayed beneath her feet. She tried to pace the tiny length of the stateroom, her sense of terrible loneliness and homesickness deepening with every moment. The moving of the ship horrified her, and the knowledge that it was taking her farther and farther from her home across the immense bottomless sea filled her with a terror akin to nothing she had ever known in her life before.

In the sickening, wearying dazzle of the few days previous to their sailing, the girl's mind had held but one thought—to go far away from the scenes of her pain; now perhaps the reaction had come, and her terror at the step she had taken appalled her. Memory, which had been thrust out of sight by the ever-present nagging pain that had blinded her to all else, now asserted its power, merciless and invincible. She pressed her hands to her head as though to blot out forever from her mind the pitiless ghosts that haunted her.

Like the wraiths that come and vanish in a nightmare, the events of her life came to her one by one—the happy childhood with her brother, their passionate devotion to each other, her grief at his departure for America, the months of struggle that had followed, sacrifices made for him, her attempts to make a living sufficient for his maintenance in America, and then—her marriage! After that, memory held no other thought but the immeasurable craving and longing that was almost madness for the voice, the touch, the sight of the man she had loved and left.

It was three days before her illness ended. Then, having begged the consent of the woman who attended her, she crept up the companion-way and out on deck, where the passengers were disporting and enjoying themselves.

She had looked forward to the time when she would regain sufficient strength to leave her prison-cell, for such she regarded her stateroom. In the strange medley of ideas which had curiously woven themselves into a maze in her mind, she had imagined that once in the open on deck she would see once more the shores of her home, Fujiyama's lofty peak[16] smiling against its celestial background, and hanging like a mirage in mid-air.

But there was no sight visible to her, as, with her hand shading her eyes, she looked out before her, save a vast, cold, pitiless waste of surging waters, jumping up to meet the sky, which smiled or glowered with its moods.

In the months that followed, Yuki met with nothing but kindness from the American theatrical manager and his wife. With them she went to China, India, the Philippines, and finally to Australia. From all these different points the American theatrical scout drew together a motley troupe of jugglers, fancy dancers, wizards, fencers, and performers of one sort and another, with which he hoped to make a larger fortune in America. He had combined business with this long pleasure trip, for he was on his bridal tour at the time.

By some remarkable intuition peculiar sometimes to the gayest and most frivolous hearted of women of the world, the wife of the theatrical manager had gained some insight into the cause of the pitiful sensitiveness and shrinking shyness of the queer little Japanese girl with the blue eyes, to whom she had taken an extravagant fancy.

She had taken Yuki under her personal charge, and sheltered and shielded the girl from the overbold scrutiny of those with whom they daily came in contact. It was many months, however, before she learned her history. In fact, it was only a few days before their departure for America, the expected great country in the west, which seemed to Yuki as far distant as the stars above her.

As the time for their departure, which had been delayed already much longer than the manager had anticipated, drew nearer, Yuki grew more depressed and restless, so that to the exaggerated fancy of the American woman she seemed to be fading away and entering into what she emphatically called "the last stages of consumption."[17]

---

[16] That is, Mount Fuji.
[17] That is, tuberculosis.

She cornered the girl relentlessly, and finally wrung from her the whole pitiful, tragic story of her life. How homesick and weary she had been ever since she had left Japan, how her heart seemed to faint whenever she thought of that final interview with her brother, and of the immeasurable longing for the man she loved, and whom she had married "for jus' liddle bid while."

All the big, romantic heart of the American woman went out to her as she took her into her arms and mingled her own honest tears with Yuki's.

"You sha'n't go to America," she said, drying her eyes with a tiny piece of lace which served as a handkerchief. "You are going right back to Japan, bag and baggage of you. I'm going with you, to see you get there O.K."

"Bud—" began Yuki, weakly.

"Never mind, now. I know he expects to sail in a week. I don't. I'm boss! See!"

XVIII.

The Season of the Cherry Blossom

In summer the fields of Japan are alive with color—burning flat lowlands shimmering with the dazzling gleam of the natane and azalea blossoms. In autumn the leaves, as well as the blossoms, have caught all the tints of heaven and earth, and in winter the gods are said to be resting after their riotous ramblings during the warm months. But in the springtime they awake, and in their lavish renewed youth bless hill and dale and meadow and forest with an abandon unlike any other time of year. It is the season of the cherry blossom, of the mating of the birds, the babbling of the brooks, and the chattering and unfolding anew of all the beauties of nature.

It was two years from the day when Jack and Yuki had married each other in the springtime. And Jack was back in Tokyo. Recalled thither by a telegram from the police headquarters, he was preparing to depart for America, where the police claimed they had positive evidence that Yuki had gone. He was staying at an American hotel in the city proper, and his heart on this day sickened and yearned for the little house only a few miles away that he longed and yet dreaded to see again.

Now that he contemplated leaving Japan, the dread possibility that Yuki might still be in the country and that he would be placing the distance of thousands and thousands of miles of land and water between them, depressed and weighed on his mind, despite the really plausible proof the police board had that she had gone to America with a theatrical company—that of the very man he himself had witnessed coaxing her to go with him.

The afternoon previous to the day set for sailing, his melancholy and morbidness grew in intensity. With no fixed purpose in view he started out from his hotel, tramped half-way across Tokyo, then hailed a jinrikisha and gave the runner orders to take him to the little house that had formerly been his home, and which he had struggled against visiting ever since his return to Tokyo.

As in a dream the interminable stretch of rice-fields, blue mountains, and valleys and hamlets, stretching away into misty outlines, flashed by him, and he noted only half absently how the heels of his runner were all worn hard just as if they had dried in the sun. Yuki once had called his attention to this.

"The honorable soles are the same," she had said. "It is the perpetual running. The gods have mercifully protected the feet from pain."

The landscape about him, familiar as the face of a mother, gave him no pain now. He was conscious only of a sense of ineffable rest and peace, as a traveler who has wandered long feels when nearing home. And soon the runner had stopped with a jerk, and was doubling over and waiting for his pay.

Should he humbly wait for his excellency to condescend to return to the city?

"Just for a little while," Jack told him absently. And he went through the little garden gate and up the pebbled adobe path, now arched on either side by two rows of cherry-blossom trees, that met at the top and made a bower under which to walk.

When he had pushed the door backward and stepped inside he paused irresolute, his heart paining him with its rapid beating. Coming from out of the blaze of the outdoor light into the shadowed room, his vision dazzled him. But gradually the objects inside grew upon his consciousness, and a rosy pain, an ecstasy that stung him with its sweetness, shot upward like a dawn through all his being.

He scarcely dared breathe, so potent was the influence of the place upon him. He feared to stir, lest the spell, ghostly and entrancing as the influence of a magic hand, might vanish into mistland, for with all the immeasurable pain that rushed to his heart in a flame was mingled a tentative, exquisite pleasure—a survival of the old joy he had once known.

And there came back to his mind whisperings of the old mysterious romances she had been wont to ramble into. What was that tale of the spirit which haunted and was felt but never seen? Was there not behind it all some mysterious possibility of such a spirit? For the very furnishings of the room, the mats, the vases, the old broken-down hammock, and his big tobacco-bon, each and all of them suddenly assumed a personality—the personality of one he loved.

Stepping on tip-toe, he crossed the room and stooped to touch the little drum, the sticks of which were snapped in twain. And then he suddenly remembered how she had broken them because he had complained one day that her drum disturbed him. He had liked the koto and the samisen; the drum she had beaten on when she mocked him. Now the sight of it beat against his brain and heart.

He could not bear the sight of those little broken sticks. He tried to cover them with his handkerchief, as if they were the evidence of a crime.

"The place is haunted!" he said, and scarce knew his own hollow voice, which the echoes of the silent room mocked back at him.

"I shall go mad," he said, and again the echoes repeated, "Mad! mad! mad!"

Then he covered his eyes, and sat in the silence, motionless and still.

From afar off there came to him the melancholy sweetness of the bells of a neighboring temple. They caused his hearing exquisite pain. What memories were recalled by them! But now every toll of the bells, slow and muffled, seemed to speak of baffled hope and despair. There was no balm in their sweet monotone. Would they never cease? Why were they so loud? They had not been so formerly. Now they filled all the land with their ringing. What were they tolling for, and, ah, why had the ghostly visitants of his house caught up the tone, and softly, sweetly, with piercing cadence, chanted back and echoed the sighing of the bells?

The house was full of music, inexpressibly dear and familiar. He started to his feet, trembling like one afflicted with ague.[18] And gradually words, in a fairy language that he had learned to love, began to form themselves into the melody of a voice.

Slowly, painfully, like one led by unseen, subtle, persuasive hands, he went forward, and up and up the spiral stairs till he had reached her chamber, and there he stood, like one who has come far and can go no farther.

One other presence besides himself was within. This he knew, and still could not comprehend. He could see her plainly, just as she had been in life—her little, shining head, her dear, small hands, the long, blue, misty eyes, and the small mouth with the little pathetic droop that had come to it in the last few days they had been together. She stood with her hands raised, dreamily loitering before a mirror, putting cherry blossoms in her hair on either side of her head. But at the prolonged silence that ensued she turned slowly about, and then she saw the man standing silently in the doorway.

She was not a girl to scream or faint, but she went gray with fear, and stood perfectly still there in the middle of the room. Then gradually her eyes traveled upward to the man's face, and there they remained transfixed.

---

[18] A fever.

"The Thousand Petals of Cherry Blossoms Were Falling About Them." From A Japanese Nightingale *by Onoto Watanna (New York: Harper and Bros., 1901). Illustrated by Genjiro Yeto.*

For a long while they faced each other thus, both with hearts that seemed not to beat. Then the man made a movement towards her, a passionate, wild movement, and she had dropped the flowers from her hands, and had gone to meet him. The next moment he was crushing her to him. When he released her but a moment, it was to hold her again and yet again, as though he feared to find her gone, and his arms empty once more, as they had been for so long. He could only breathe her name—"Yuki! Yuki! My wife! My wife!"

Neither tried to explain. There was time enough for that. They were absorbed alone in the fact that they were together at last.

Someone noisily entered the house and whirled up the stairs. It was the American girl. She gazed in upon them with eyes and mouth agape in amazement.

"Well, I never!" she ejaculated, and went out and down the steps, sobbing aloud.

"Such a romance! Such a nice, big fellow, too! And, oh, dear me, I've lost her sure enough now forever! Bother men, anyhow!" and she jumped into Jack's jinrikisha and bade the man take her on the instant to Tokyo.

Meanwhile the lovers had wandered out into the open air. He was holding both her hands in his, and his eyes were straying hungrily over her face; her eyes bewitched him; her lips thrilled him.

The thousand petals of cherry blossoms were falling about them and the birds had all flown to their garden and were twittering and bursting their little throats with melody. A fugitive wind came up from the bay and tossed the little scattering curls about her ears and temples. A strand of her hair swept across his hand. He stooped and kissed it reverently, and she laughed and thrilled under the touch of his lips.

"I love you with all my soul," he said. "Do not laugh at me now."

She said, "Dear my lord, I will never laugh more ad you. I laugh only for the joy ad being with you."

"I will take you to my home," he said.

"I will follow you to the end of the world and beyond," said she.

"And we will come back here again, love. We will take up the broken threads of our lives and piece them together."

"They shall never again be broken," she said. But he must needs spoil her divine faith. "Till death do us part," he added.

"No, no. We will have the faith of our simple peasant folk. We are wedded for ever an' ever."

"Yes, forever," he repeated.

Appendix: Madame Butterfly *and* A Japanese Nightingale, *Synopses of the Plays*

MADAME BUTTERFLY: *A Tragedy of Japan* by David Belasco
Opened at the New York Herald Square Theatre, January 8, 1900.

Cho-Cho-San	Blanche Bates
Suzuki	Marie Bates
Mr. Sharpless	Claude Gillingwater
Lieutenant B. F. Pinkerton	Frank Worthing
Yamadori	Albert Bruning
Nakodo	E. P. Wilks
Kate (Pinkerton's wife)	Katherine Black
Trouble	Little Kittie
Attendant	William Lamp
Attendant	Westropp Saunders

The play opens two years after Pinkerton's departure, with Cho-Cho-San praying to the goddess Shaka for his return. Unknown to her, Pinkerton has returned the day before and his American wife is waiting in Nagasaki for him. Cho-Cho-San and Suzuki make plans for what they will do when they spot his ship in the harbor, visible from their house on Higashi Hill overlooking Nakasaki Bay. For Suzuki Cho-Cho-San play-acts what she imagines the homecoming will be like. Sharpless, the American consul, appears at their door, accompanied by the *nakodo*, or marriage broker. Sharpless tells her that Pinkerton has written to him, prompting his visit. Cho-Cho-San assumes he has written to ask about her, and she tells Sharpless of her great love for her American husband, the story of her samurai father's suicide, and her rejection of the nakoda's marriage offer from a Japanese businessman, Yamadori. Yamadori appears with two attendants, pressing his suit again. Sharpless discusses American marriage customs and divorce laws at Cho-Cho-San's request. Sharpless reads Pinkerton's letter to Cho-Cho-San, informing her that Pinkerton does not consider himself married to her. Their child, Trouble, wanders in, and Sharpless is disturbed to see that there is such a child. He and Yamadori leave.

Hearing the ship's guns from the harbor, Cho-Cho-San excitedly anticipates Pinkerton's return, despite Sharpless's words, and she and Suzuki prepare for his homecoming. For fourteen minutes of actual stage time, there is no dialogue as she waits through the night for Pinkerton to show up. The next morning, Suzuki leaves to prepare breakfast and Cho-Cho-San departs from the room. Pinkerton enters with Sharpless, looking for her. Sharpless, seeing the nakodo, admonishes him for telling Pinkerton's wife about the baby and his relationship with Cho-Cho-San. The nakodo explains that he hoped the news would prompt Pinkerton to break off with Cho-Cho-San, thus freeing her to marry Yamadori. Pinkerton's wife, Kate, has offered to take the child if Pinkerton speaks with Cho-Cho-San. Hearing Cho-Cho-San about to enter, Pinkerton loses his courage and leaves.

Sharpless gives her some money Pinkerton has brought for her and does not tell her that he wants to take the baby away. Kate enters the room looking for her husband and takes the distraught Cho-Cho-San in her arms to comfort her. Kate asks her if they can take the baby to America as that would be the best thing for him. Cho-Cho-San reluctantly agrees and asks her to return in fifteen minutes to take him away. After Kate leaves the room, Cho-Cho-San asks Suzuki to leave also. Suzuki pushes the baby into the room and Cho-Cho-San takes him in her arms, then goes behind a screen to put her father's sword to her neck. Appearing from behind the screen with her wound, she takes the baby in her arms again. Kate appears with Pinkerton behind her. Pinkerton kneels in grief and embraces Cho-Cho-San and the baby. She dies in his arms.

A JAPANESE NIGHTINGALE BY WILLIAM YOUNG
Opened at the New York Daly Theater, November 20, 1903.*

Yuki	Margaret Illington
Jack Bigelow	Orrin Johnson
Mr. Harker of California	Eugene Jepson
Theodosia Harker	Olive May
Bobby Newcome, navy ensign	Fritz Williams
Mr. Hammond, U.S. consul	Frank Gillmore
Taro Jokichi (Yuki's brother)	Vincent Serrano
Nekko, of the Imperial Council	Robert McWade Jr.
Ido, the marriage broker	Frederick Perry
Kayo-San, Yuki's maid	May Buckley
Yuki's Japanese stepmother	Miriam Hutchins
Maru-San	Fanny Marinoff
Songs and dances by Saburo Arai	

The American consul in Tokyo, Mr. Hammond, arranges for Jack Bigelow to marry Yuki against his better judgment, and the marriage license is held in his office. Nekko, the villain of the play, is a wealthy Japanese businessman who disapproves of foreign marriages and jealously plots to make Yuki his own wife. He sends agents to kill the consul, burn his books, and steal the wedding certificate, all of which transpire in the first scenes. Yuki is warned that Jack will be murdered next if she does not abandon him and retire to a Buddhist temple. This she does, and Jack's former classmate at Yale, Taro, who unbeknownst to Jack until this moment is Yuki's brother, unexpectedly and angrily confronts him. Taro is bent on revenge for what he believes is Jack's seduction of his sister unless Jack can produce the marriage certificate.

Californians Theodosia Harker and her father arrive on the scene and, with an American ensign named Bobby Newcome, track down the evil Nekko, kill him in self-defense when Nekko attacks them with a knife, and recover the wedding certificate. Meanwhile, Yuki is still at the Buddhist temple, and in the third act, performs the Bon Odori dance with lines of women in clinging robes. She returns of her own volition to her marital home where she finds Bigelow and is reunited with him.

---

*There is no extant version of this play. The plot summary here is a sketchy and incomplete summation of news accounts of the play.

Glossary

Note: The romanization of Japanese words in the text is not consistent with contemporary spellings of Japanese words but have been maintained as they were used by Long and Eaton.

andon	lantern with paper shade
ayah	Hindu term for nursemaid
barbarian	Japanese term (translated) for a Westerner, primarily used in the nineteenth century
biwa	Japanese drum
Dai-Butsu	a very large, famous statue of a seated Buddha constructed in 1252, located in Kamakura, Japan, about twenty miles south of Tokyo
"egspeg"	expect
"ezag"	exactly
fusuma	sliding doors used in Japanese houses, constructed of light wooden frames with opaque paper panels
"hade"	head
hibachi	small charcoal grill or burner
"hoarry"	hurry
"hoash"	hush
ichi ban	"the best"
jinrikisha	two-wheeled carriage pulled by a human runner
joshi	possibly an incorrect transliteration of the Japanese word for suicide, *jisatsu*
kaimyo	term used for Buddhist believers who have passed into the afterlife, as well as the namecards of the dead hung at shrines where the living pray to their ancestors
kanzashi	two-pronged hair comb
kazoku	Japanese nobility
kimono	traditional Japanese gown, tied at the waist by a tightly wrapped cummerbund called an *obi*
"Kirishitan"	Christian
koro	vase
koto	zither-like instrument

kurumma	like a *jinrikisha*, a carriage pulled by human runners
Kwannon	the Buddhist goddess of mercy
"lig"	like
"loog"	look
look-at meeting	meeting arranged by the *nakodo* between the prospective bride and groom where the couple are allowed to "look at" each other, often for the first time. Although they may exchange pleasantries, the couple are not allowed to discuss the impending marriage or their feelings regarding the match.
Meido	Buddhist land of the dead
ménage	a French term for household
Mikado	Emperor of Japan
mousmee, mousmè	young Japanese woman. The term carried with it the implication that the woman was unmarried and thus sexually available.
nakodo	marriage broker
natane	rapeseed
"nob'y"	nobody
obi	sash worn with a kimono, the ornamentation of which corresponded with the importance and wealth of the wearer
oku-san	wife. Eaton transliterated the Japanese as "okusama."
omeshi	clothing; in the story's context, a sash
"oogly"	ugly
"raddle"	rattled
"recomleck"	recollect
sake	Japanese rice wine, served hot or cold
samisen	Japanese stringed instrument like a guitar with an elongated neck and three strings
samurai, samourai	Japanese military caste and members of that caste
sayonara	good-bye
sen	Japanese monetary unit; one-hundreth of a *yen*. In the texts it is meant to be the equivalent of an American penny.
Shaka	name for Sakyamuni Gautama Buddha (also known as Siddhartha); used by the Japanese Tendai sect of Buddhists
shoji	sliding paper screens or panels
"thing"	think
tobacco-bon	pipe and tobacco pouch
tokonama	chest of drawers
tokonoma	alcove reserved for a beautiful object found in most Japanese homes

woman of joy	euphemism for a prostitute
yen	basic unit of Japanese currency. At the time Long and Eaton were writing, 100 yen equaled approximately 20 dollars.
yujo	prostitute
zashishi	living room or parlor

Bibliography

WORKS BY JOHN LUTHER LONG
Many manuscripts are held in the John Luther Long Papers at the Harry Ransom
Humanities Research Center, University of Texas–Austin.

Novels and Short Story Collections
1895   *Miss Cherry Blossom of Tokyo*. Philadelphia: J. B. Lippincott Co.
1898   *Madame Butterfly. Purple Eyes. A Gentleman of Japan. Kito. Glory*. New
       York: Century.
       "Madame Butterfly." *The Century Illustrated Magazine* 55 (January):
       274–292.
1900   *The Fox-Woman*. Philadelphia: J. B. Lippincott.
1901   *Prince of Illusion. Dolce. Ein Nix-Nutz. The Honorable Christmas Gift of
       Yoshida Aramidzu. Dizzy Dave. The Horse Trade. Jane an' Me. The Dream
       Woman*. New York: Century.
1902   *Naughty Nan*. New York: Century. Originally published in *Lippincott's* 69
       (January 1902): 3–87.
1903   *Sixty Jane. The Strike on the Schlafeplatz Railroad. Our Anchel. The Lady
       and Her Soul. The Beautiful Graveyard. Lucky Jim. The Outrageous Miss
       Dawn-Dream. The Little House in the Little Street Where the Sun Never
       Came. The Atonement*. New York: Century.
1903   *Madame Butterfly* (first book edition). New York: Century.
1904   *Little Miss Joy-Sing*. Philadelphia: H. Altemus.
1905   *Seffy*. Indianapolis: Bobbs-Merrill.
1905   *Heimweh. The Siren. The Loaded Gun. Liebereich. Iupiter Tonans. Sis.
       Thor's Emerald. Guile*. New York: Macmillan.
1906   *The Way of the Gods*. New York: Grosset and Dunlap.
1908   *Felice*. New York: Moffat, Yard & Co.
1912   *Baby Grand. Tom, Dick and Harry—Et Caetera. Spilled Milk. Dull Jim.
       Dolly Jack. The Little Lady Who Wouldn't Spoil Christmas*. Boston: R. G.
       Badger.
1913   *War; or, What Happens When One Loves One's Enemy*. Indianapolis:
       Bobbs-Merrill.

WORKS BY WINNIFRED EATON
Works are listed in order of publication. The Winnifred Eaton Reeve Fonds at the
University of Calgary contain many unpublished manuscripts, including several au-
tobiographical pieces and dozens of screenplays.

Novels
1899   *Miss Numè of Japan: A Japanese-American Romance*. Chicago: Rand,
       McNally.

1901   *A Japanese Nightingale.* New York: Harper and Bros.
1902   *The Wooing of Wistaria.* New York: Harper and Bros.
1903   *The Heart of Hyacinth.* New York: Harper and Bros.
1904   *The Love of Azalea.* New York: Dodd, Mead and Co.
1904   *Daughters of Nijo.* New York: Macmillan.
1906   *A Japanese Blossom.* New York: Harper and Bros.
1907   *The Diary of Delia: Being a Veracious Chronicle of the Kitchen with Some
        Side-Lights on the Parlour.* New York: Doubleday, Page, and Co. Serialized
        in *The Saturday Evening Post.*
1910   *Tama.* New York: Harper and Bros.
1912   *The Honorable Miss Moonlight.* New York: Harper and Bros.
1915   *Me: A Book of Remembrance.* New York: Century. Originally published in
        Century Magazine, 1915.
1916   *Marion: The Story of an Artist's Model.* New York: W. J. Watt. Originally
        serialized in *Hearst's Magazine*, 1916.
1922   *Sunny-San.* New York: George H. Doran Co.
1924   *Cattle.* New York: A. L. Burt Co.
1925   *His Royal Nibs.* New York: W. J. Watt.

OTHER SOURCES CONSULTED

Ammons, Elizabeth. *Conflicting Stories: American Women Writers at the Turn into the
    Twentieth Century.* New York: Oxford University Press, 1992.
Bacon, Alice Mabel. *Japanese Girls and Women.* 1891; Revised and enlarged edition,
    Boston: Houghton Mifflin & Co., 1902.
Baker, Houston. *Modernism and the Harlem Renaissance.* Chicago: University of
    Chicago Press, 1987.
Bederman, Gail. *Manliness and Civilization: A Cultural History of Gender and Race
    in the United States, 1880–1917.* Chicago: University of Chicago Press, 1995.
Belasco, David. *Six Plays.* Boston: Little, Brown, and Co., 1928.
Birchall, Diana. *Onoto Watanna: The Story of Winnifred Eaton.* Urbana: University of
    Illinois Press, 2001.
Carby, Hazel. *Reconstructing Womanhood: The Emergence of the Afro-American
    Woman Novelist.* New York: Oxford University Press, 1987.
Chamberlain, Basil Hall. *Things Japanese.* 5th ed. London: J. Murray, 1905.
Chan, Jeffery Paul; Frank Chin; Lawson Fusao Inada; and Shawn Wong, eds. *The Big
    Aiiieeeee!: An Anthology of Chinese American and Japanese American Literature.*
    New York: Meridian, 1991.
Chisolm, Lawrence. *Fenollosa: The Far East and American Culture.* New Haven:
    Yale University Press, 1963.
Chuman, Frank F. *The Bamboo People: Japanese-Americans, Their History and the
    Law.* Chicago: Japanese American Research Project, Japanese American Citizens
    League, 1981.
Cole, Jean Lee. *The Literary Voices of Winnifred Eaton: Redefining Ethnicity and Au-
    thenticity.* New Brunswick, N.J.: Rutgers University Press, 2002.
Downer, Lesley. *Women of the Pleasure Quarters: The Secret History of the Geisha.*
    New York: Broadway Books, 2001.
Doyle, James. "Sui Sin Far and Onoto Watanna: Two Early Chinese-Canadian Au-
    thors." *Canadian Literature* 140 (Spring 1994): 50–58.

Dulles, Foster Rhea. *Yankees and Samurai: America's Role in the Emergence of Modern Japan.* New York: Harper & Row, 1965.

Eaton, Edith (Sui Sin Far). *Mrs. Spring Fragrance and Other Stories (1912),* ed. Amy Ling and Annette White-Parks. Bloomington: Indiana University Press, 1995.

Ferens, Dominika. *Edith and Winnifred Eaton: The Uses of Ethnography in Turn-of-the-Century Asian American Literature.* Urbana: University of Illinois Press, 2002.

Fields, Rick. "'No Oblivion in the Orange Poppy': Ernest Fenollosa and Turn of the Century Orientalism." *Zero* 4 (1980): 8–24.

Hattori, Tomo. "Model Minority Discourse and Asian American Jouis-Sense." *differences* 11.2 (1999): 228–247.

Hayot, Eric. "Critical Dreams: Orientalism, Modernism, and the Meaning of Pound's China." *Twentieth Century Literature* 45 (Winter 1999): 511–533.

Hearn, Lafcadio. *Exotics and Retrospectives.* Boston: Little, Brown, and Co., 1898.

——. *Glimpses of Unfamiliar Japan.* 2 vols. Boston: Houghton Mifflin Company, 1894.

——. *Japan, an Attempt at Interpretation.* New York: Macmillan, 1904.

——. *Out of the East: Reveries and Studies of New Japan.* Boston: Houghton Mifflin Co., 1895.

Henning, Joseph M. *Outposts of Civilization: Race, Religion, and the Formative Years of American-Japanese Relations.* New York: NYU Press, 2000.

Hwang, David Henry. *M. Butterfly.* New York: Plume/Penguin, 1986.

Iriye, Akira. *Pacific Estrangement: Japanese and American Expansion, 1897–1911.* Cambridge, Mass.: Harvard University Press, 1972.

Jones, Gavin. *Strange Talk: The Politics of Dialect Literature in Gilded Age America.* Berkeley and Los Angeles: University of California Press, 1999.

Kaplan, Amy, and Donald E. Pease, eds. *Cultures of United States Imperialism.* Durham, N.C.: Duke University Press, 1993.

Kauffmann, Stanley. "Two Vulgar Geniuses: Augustin Daly and David Belasco." *Yale Review* 76(4) (Summer 1987): 496–513.

Kim, Elaine H. *Asian American Literature: An Introduction to the Writings and Their Social Context.* Philadelphia: Temple University Press, 1982.

Krapp, George Philip. *The English Language in America.* New York: Century, 1925.

Kunst, Arthur E. *Lafcadio Hearn.* New York: Twayne, 1969.

LaFeber, Walter. *The Clash: A History of U.S.-Japan Relations.* New York: W. W. Norton, 1997.

Lape, Noreen Grover. "Bartered Brides and Compulsory Bachelors on the Asian-American Frontiers: The Marriage Fiction of Sui Sin Far and Onoto Watanna." In "West of the Border: Cultural Liminality in the Literature of the Western American Frontiers," 177–275. Ph.D. diss., Temple University, 1996.

Lears, T. J. Jackson. *No Place of Grace: Antimodernism and the Transformation of American Culture 1880–1920.* New York: Pantheon, 1981.

Lee, Rachel. *The Americas of Asian American Literature: Gendered Fictions of Nation and Transnation.* Princeton, N.J.: Princeton University Press, 1999.

Lee, Robert. *Orientals: Asian Americans in Popular Culture.* Philadelphia: Temple University Press, 1999.

Lim, Shirley Geok-lin, and Amy Ling, eds. *Reading the Literatures of Asian America.* Philadelphia: Temple University Press, 1992.

Ling, Amy. *Between Worlds: Women Writers of Chinese Ancestry.* New York: Pergamon Press, 1990.

———. "Chinese American Women Writers: The Tradition behind Maxine Hong Kingston." In *Redefining American Literary History,* ed. A. LaVonne Ruoff and Jerry Ward, Jr., 219-236. New York: Modern Literature Association, 1990.

———. "Creating One's Self: The Eaton Sisters." In *Reading the Literatures of Asian America,* ed. Shirley Geok-Lin Lim and Amy Ling, 305-318. Philadelphia: Temple University Press, 1992.

———. "Revelation and Mask: Autobiographies of the Eaton Sisters." *A/B Auto/Biography Studies* 3:2 (Summer 1987): 49.

———. "Winnifred Eaton: Ethnic Chameleon and Popular Success." *MELUS* 11:3 (1984): 5–15.

Ling, Jinqi. *Narrating Nationalisms: Ideology and Form in Asian American Literature.* New York: Oxford University Press, 1998.

Little, Frances. *The Lady of the Decoration.* New York: Century, 1906.

Loti, Pierre. *Madame Crysanthème* (1887). Trans. Laura Ensor. Rutland, Vt.: Charles E. Tuttle Co., 1973.

Lowe, Lisa. *Immigrant Acts: Asian American Cultural Politics.* Durham, N.C.: Duke University Press, 1996.

Lyman, Stanford M. *The Asian in North America.* Santa Barbara, Calif.: ABC-CLIO, 1970.

Marchetti, Gina. *Romance and the "Yellow Peril": Race, Sex, and Discursive Strategies in Hollywood Fiction.* Berkeley and Los Angeles: University of California Press, 1993.

Matsukawa, Yuko. "Cross-Dressing and Cross-Naming: Decoding Onoto Watanna." In *Tricksterism in Turn-of-the-Century U.S. Literature,* ed. Elizabeth Ammons and Annette White-Parks, 106-125. Hanover: University Press of New England, 1994.

Meech, Julia, and Gabriel P. Weisberg, eds. *Japonisme Comes to America: The Japanese Impact on the Graphic Arts 1876–1925.* New York: Abrams, 1990.

Moser, Linda Trinh. Afterword to *Me: A Book of Remembrance* (1915), by Winnifed Eaton, 357-372. Jackson: University of Mississippi Press, 1998.

———. "Chinese Prostitutes, Japanese Geishas, and Working Women: Images of Race, Class, and Gender in the Work of Edith Eaton/Sui Sin Far and Winnifred Eaton/Onoto Watanna." Ph.D. diss., University of California at Davis, 1997.

Moy, James. *Marginal Sights: Staging the Chinese in America.* Iowa City: University of Iowa Press, 1993.

Murray, Paul. *A Fantastic Journey: The Life and Literature of Lafcadio Hearn.* Ann Arbor: University of Michigan Press, 1993.

Najmi, Samina. Introduction to *The Heart of Hyacinth,* by Onoto Watanna [Winnifred Eaton], v-xlvi. Seattle: University of Washington Press, 2000.

———. "Racio-Cultural Fludity as Rebellion in Onoto Watanna's *The Heart of Hyacinth.*" In "Representations of White Women in Works by Selected African American and Asian American Authors," 126–158. Ph.D. diss., Tufts University, 1997.

Noguchi, Yone. *The Story of Yone Noguchi: Told by Himself.* Philadelphia: George W. Jacobs, 1915.

Ohmann, Richard. *Selling Culture: Magazines, Markets, and Class at the Turn of the Century.* New York: Verso Press, 1996.

Oishi, Eve. Introduction to *Miss Numè of Japan* (1899), by Winnifred Eaton, xii–xxxi. Baltimore: Johns Hopkins University Press, 1999.

Okihiro, Gary. *Common Ground: Reimagining American History*. Princeton, N.J.: Princeton University Press, 2001.

Omi, Michael, and Howard Winant. *Racial Formation in the United States: From the 1960s to the 1980s*. New York: Routledge and Kegan Paul, 1986.

Qian, Zhaoming. *Orientalism and Modernism: The Legacy of China in Pound and Williams*. Durham, N.C.: Duke University Press, 1995.

Radway, Janice. *Reading the Romance: Women, Patriarchy, and Popular Literature*. Chapel Hill: University of North Carolina Press, 1984.

Rosenstone, Robert. *A Mirror in the Shrine: American Encounters with Meiji Japan*. Cambridge, Mass.: Harvard University Press, 1988.

Said, Edward. *Orientalism*. New York: Pantheon, 1976.

Sawada, Mitziko. *Tokyo Life, New York Dreams: Urban Japanese Visions of America, 1890–1924*. Berkeley and Los Angeles: University of California Press, 1996.

Schueller, Malini Johar. *U.S. Orientalisms: Race, Nation, and Gender in Literature, 1790–1890*. Ann Arbor: University of Michigan Press, 1998.

Shea, Pat. "Winnifred Eaton and the Politics of Miscegenation in Popular Fiction," *MELUS* 22:2 (Summer 1997): 19ff. (electronic format).

Solberg, S. E. "Sui Sin Far/Edith Eaton: First Chinese-American Fictionist." *MELUS* 8.1 (1981): 27–39.

Sollors, Werner. *Beyond Ethnicity: Consent and Descent in American Culture*. New York: Oxford University Press, 1986.

Spaulding, Carol Vivian. "Turning Japanese: Ethnic Improvisation in the Work of Winnifred Eaton/Onoto Watanna." In "Blue-Eyed Asians: Eurasianism in the Work of Edith Eaton/Sui Sin Far, Winnifred Eaton/Onoto Watanna, and Diana Chang," 164–248. Ph.D. diss., University of Iowa, 1996.

Stevenson, Elizabeth. *The Grass Lark: A Study of Lafcadio Hearn*. New Brunswick, N.J.: Transaction Press, 1999.

Sundquist, Eric. *To Wake the Nations: Race in the Making of American Literature*. Cambridge, Mass.: Belknap Press/Harvard University Press, 1993.

Takaki, Ronald. *Iron Cages: Race and Culture in Nineteenth-Century America*. New York: Knopf, 1979.

———. *Strangers from a Different Shore: A History of Asian Americans*. Boston: Little, Brown, 1989.

Tchen, John Kuo Wei. *New York before Chinatown: Orientalism and the Shaping of American Culture, 1776–1882*. Baltimore: Johns Hopkins University Press, 1999.

Tompkins, Jane. *Sensational Designs: The Cultural Work of American Fiction, 1790–1860*. New York: Oxford University Press, 1985.

Van Rij, Jan. *Madame Butterfly: Japonisme, Puccini, and the Search for the Real Cho-Cho-San*. Berkeley: Stone Bridge Press, 2001.

Wald, Patricia. *Constituting Americans: Cultural Anxiety and Narrative Form*. Durham, N.C.: Duke University Press, 1995.

White-Parks, Annette. *Sui Sin Far/Edith Maude Eaton: A Literary Biography*. Urbana: University of Illinois Press, 1995.

Wilkinson, Endymion. *Japan versus the West: Image and Reality*. London: Penguin, 1990.

Woo, Min-Seong. "Gendered Geography between East and West: Madame Butterfly Narrative as the Dominant Representation of Asian Women in the West." Ph.D. diss., University of Wisconsin, Madison, 1997. Dissertation Abstract no.

DA9810367. Ann Arbor, Mich.: Dissertation Abstracts International, A. 59(2) (1998): 376.

Wordell, Charles B. *Japan's Image in America: Popular Writing about Japan, 1800–1941*. Tokyo: Yamaguchi Publishing House, 2000.

Wu, William F. *The Yellow Peril: Chinese Americans in American Fiction 1850–1940*. Hamden, Conn.: Archon Books, 1982.

Yoshihara, Mari. "In Search of Mrs. Pinkerton." Unpublished manuscript.

Yu, Beongcheon. *The Great Circle: American Writers and the Orient*. Detroit: Wayne State University Press, 1983.